Narcissists

The Ultimate Guide to Understanding Narcissism and Ways of Dealing With a Narcissist Who Is Using Manipulation at Work or in an Abusive Relationship

Contents

Contents

Introduction

Narcissism is a hot topic right now. Everyone seems to be talking about it, and there are tons of books being published on the topic. What makes this book different from the other books out there? Many hours of research have gone into this book, and it contains the latest information. More than that, this book is not about teaching you how to diagnose a narcissist clinically, but instead, it is about showing you how you can identify the narcissists in your life.

Narcissists can cause unseen damage. They are masters of disguise. They make us feel that we are safe and loved in the beginning, only to turn on us and cause us pain. Maybe you have someone in your life that you think may be a narcissist. Maybe you are wondering if a specific person in your life displays narcissistic tendencies.

It can be hard to identify a narcissist by their behavior early on in a relationship. They can come across as confident and motivated. They can be extremely successful, which can make it hard to believe that they are narcissists or that they could abuse you.

Growing up with a narcissist in your family can make you feel as if you have nowhere to turn. You may feel that they can convince everyone else that *you* are the problem. They can make you feel that you are completely alone. By identifying the narcissist, you are going to be able to take the control back from them, and that is exactly what you are going to learn how to do in this book.

Narcissists thrive on being in control. They want someone in their life that is going to do exactly what they say right when they say it. How do they find these people? How does a narcissist choose their target? By understanding the answers to these questions, you will be able to protect yourself from narcissists now and in the future.

This book was created with you in mind. So many people want to focus on the narcissist; they seem to be obsessed with what motivates a narcissist and want to know the inner workings of the narcissist's brain. I feel that we should focus on the person that the narcissist targets. Ensuring that you are no longer the victim of a narcissist and helping you to move forward with your life is much more important and much more fascinating than why a narcissist does what they do.

Throughout this book, you will hear stories of Todd and Stacy. Todd is a narcissist; Stacy is his partner. You will see how Stacy was able to identify Todd's behavior and start protecting herself from his abusive tendencies. You will learn how you can do that as well.

Most importantly, you will learn what to do if you are the victim of a narcissist, how you can move forward with your life, and where you can find help.

Chapter One: Understanding Personality

"She has such a great personality." Have you ever heard someone say this? Maybe you have said it yourself. It is something that most people say regularly, but what is personality? Personality does not have one single definition.

In 1950 Raymond Cattell stated that personality is what allows us to predict what someone is going to do in any given situation.

In 1999 Walter Mischel described personality as the pattern of a person's behavior, which includes their thoughts, their feelings, their actions, and their emotions.

There are many other definitions of personality out there, but one thing that all of them have in common is the idea that a person's personality is made up of the constant behavior that they display. For example, if you are pleasant all of the time, people will describe you as having a pleasant personality.

Every day, we assess different types of personalities. Personality Psychology does this as well; it is the scientific study of what makes you, you. Personality Psychology is about understanding how a person's personality develops, as well as how their personality influences them as a person.

The personality is something that comes from within you. Of course, personality can be influenced by genetics, the environment in which a person grows up, and their life experiences.

The most widely accepted theory of personality is the "Big Five." According to the Big Five Theory, every person's personality is made up of five traits which include:

1. Extraversion, or how socially confident you are.

2. Agreeableness, or enjoyable pleasance.

3. Neuroticism and mental health.

4. Conscientiousness, which means how well a person wants to do something, or how seriously they take their obligations.

5. Openness or frankness.

Each trait is one factor of the spectrum, and according to this theory, every personality can be found within that spectrum. An example of this may be that you fall high on the spectrum in conscientiousness and agreeableness, while being in the middle in extroversion and openness, and being low in neuroticism. Every personality can be categorized by using these traits.

Freud believed that personality is developed at a very young age. According to his theory, certain stages need to be gone through for the personality to develop. As a person successfully completes one stage, they move on to the next. However, if the stage was not completed, that would affect their personality for the rest of their lives.

On the other hand, Erik Erikson believed that if a person completed all of the stages of personality development, they would form a healthy personality. While Freud believed that once your personality was developed, you were stuck with it, Erikson believed that it would continue to develop throughout your lifetime.

Have you ever taken a personality test? There are many different types of personality tests out there, and chances are that you have come across one or two in your lifetime. Many of us have taken personality tests when we are applying for jobs. Perhaps you took one when you were in high school, to determine what type of job you should do in the future. Or maybe you took them online as a form of entertainment.

Learning more about your personality is going to allow you to understand why you do the things that you do, why you feel certain ways, and why you work better with some people than others.

If you are taking online personality tests, bear in mind that some of these tests can help you learn a little bit about yourself, and they are fun to do; however, you should not rely on them for any type of diagnosis. If you think that you or someone that you know is suffering from a personality disorder, a formal diagnosis should be made by a personality psychologist.

A personality disorder is a mental disorder that impacts your thoughts, your interpersonal functioning, and your behaviors. At the time of this writing, there are ten personality disorders, including antisocial personality disorder, obsessive-compulsive personality disorder, narcissistic personality disorder, and more.

Being told that you have a personality disorder can be very upsetting, but there is help available for those that want it. When you work with a mental health professional, you are going to begin to understand the difficulties that personality disorders can cause for you, and you are going to start learning coping skills.

The majority of us strive to be good people. However, we find that the world that we live in seems obsessed with learning about those who don't. Psychopaths and narcissists are all the rage. People watch movies and television shows about them, and they seem to fascinate many people.

People like narcissists and psychopaths rank high on the dark triad spectrum. The dark triad spectrum consists of negative traits that any person may possess. Those include Machiavellianism, which means manipulating other people; narcissism, which means that they expect special treatment or admiration; and psychopathy, which means that they are insensitive or callous.

It is this dark triad that constitutes the dark parts of our personality. On the other end of the spectrum is the light triad, comprised of traits that are in contrast to those of the dark triad. These include humanism, or valuing each person and their dignity; Kantianism, which means that you do not set out to use a person; and faith in humanity, which simply means that you believe people are inherently good.

When a person scores high on the dark triad, they generally are unsatisfied with their life, and may display some psycho-social behaviors such as violence, aggression, or low empathy. Those that score higher on the light triad tend to be happier in life, more successful, adept at getting along with other people, and contributing to society.

In all of us exists some light and some dark. Not one single person is going to be all light or all dark. We have to be careful of those that are more dark than light. They are the ones that will exploit, dominate, or abuse you.

While it is the job of personality psychologists to research and understand personality, it is good for everyone to understand a little bit about it. Understanding personality is going to help you better understand yourself, as well as those around you.

Chapter Two: What Narcissism Is and How to Identify It

Narcissism is characterized by an exaggerated sense of self-worth and a lack of empathy for other people. The narcissist lacks empathy, displays arrogant behavior, and has a deep need for an excessive amount of attention from other people.

While these are the most common traits of narcissism, there are so many traits that identifying narcissism can be quite complicated. There is no medical test that can be taken to determine if a person is narcissistic; psychologists must observe the behavior of people, their attitudes, and the way that they react to certain situations.

For a person to be identified as narcissistic, they must exhibit at least 55% of the following characteristics:

- **Feeling that they are superior to everyone else and having a sense of entitlement.**

The narcissist is only going to be happy when they are identified as the best, the smartest, the most competent, and the one in control. They want everything to be done their way and believe that their way is the best way. What many people fail to realize is that a narcissist can also get that feeling of superiority from being the sickest, the most injured, the victim, the most upset, the one that has been most wronged, or the one that is the worst off in life. This allows them to enjoy basking in the concern of other people.

• **Having a constant need for validation as well as attention.**

The narcissist needs attention constantly. They may follow you around the house as you are trying to do your chores, demanding your attention, or they may say something off the wall as a means of grabbing your attention. They want everyone to focus on them as much as possible. When it comes to validation, a narcissistic person cannot get this from themselves; they have to have it from other people. You can spend all of your time telling them how much you care about them, how proud of them that you are, and that you really admire them, but that will never be enough. They must have a constant stream of this validation. This is because while they are very self-absorbed and seem like they are extremely secure, deep down, they are actually insecure and feel as if they are not as good as other people. They need constant praise to feed their egos so that they do not feel like they are not measuring up.

• **Perfectionism.**

The narcissistic person has a deep desire for everything everywhere to be perfect. They expect themselves to be perfect as well as you, any event that happens in their lives, their finances, and every other detail in their lives. We all know that perfectionism is impossible, except for the narcissist. They put these high demands on themselves as well as those around them every day. When they or the people around them do not measure up, they are left feeling miserable and dissatisfied with life. This will lead to them complaining about their life or the people in it.

- **Needing to control everything.**

Narcissists are perfectionists - they want to be in control of everything in their lives. They believe that they are smarter than everyone else around them, and by being in control of everything, they will finally be able to be perfect. It is also their sense of entitlement that makes them feel that they should be able to control everything. When they are not in control or things do not work out as they had planned, they become extremely upset, which is why they demand that you do things their way. The only way that things are going to work out the way that they want them to is if you follow their script. In their mind, you are nothing more than a character playing a part in their lives. You do not have your own feelings, thoughts, or ideas.

- **Refusing to take responsibility for their actions.**

They will blame other people. While they want to be in control of everything that happens, they do not want to take any responsibility for the results, unless of course, things work out the way that they want them to. When things don't work out according to their plan, they want to place the blame on you or someone else in their lives because they feel less than perfect, and as we have already learned, a narcissist wants to be perfect. They feel that by blaming someone else for the failure, they are still perfect.

- **Being unreasonable.**

If you have ever known a narcissist, you have probably found yourself trying to reason with them at one point or another. Perhaps you tried to show the narcissist that they were causing you pain with their behavior. Deep down, you want to believe that if they can understand the pain that they are causing you, they will change. To the narcissist, your explanations make no sense. They are unable to accept that you have your own feelings and thoughts. They may tell you that they understand what you are telling them, but the truth is they really don't. The narcissist will continue to make their decisions based off of their own thoughts and feelings. For example, if they want a new car because it makes them feel good when they are driving it, they are going to get it. They are not going to consider the budget. They will not sit down and think about how their decision is going to affect you or the rest of the family. They only think about how that car makes them feel. They spend their time looking for things or people outside of themselves to fulfill a hole within themselves. They expect that everyone else just goes along with whatever they decide to do. If you don't, they can become irrational.

- **Splitting everything into good and bad.**

For a narcissist, anything negative is going to be your fault or the fault of someone else. For example, if they didn't get the promotion at work, it is because no one sees how hard they work. On the other hand, if something positive happens, they will take all of the credit for it. For example, if you worked hard to pay off all of the debt that the two of you had incurred, they may tell people that the debt was paid off because *they* worked so many extra hours.

- **Not being able to weigh the good and the bad of their decisions.**

Similar to the last example, if the narcissist wants to purchase a new car, they are not going to take the monthly payments into account. They are not going to worry about the family not having food on the table because they are focused on the way the car makes them feel.

On the other hand, they may focus completely on the negative. For example, Tom decided that he was going to go to the beach for his vacation. It rained the entire week that he was there. Tom ended up giving the hotel a terrible review because he was so angry about the weather. It did not matter that the hotel did everything within their power to ensure that his stay was a pleasant one. He felt that it was their fault that the vacation was ruined.

- **Having a deep-seated fear of rejection.**

Narcissists are terrified that they are going to be wronged or rejected. They are afraid of being ridiculed, being emotionally hurt, being seen as inadequate, or being abandoned, which is why a narcissist is unable to trust other people. The closer you become to a narcissist, the less they are going to trust you. They refuse to be vulnerable because they know that this will allow you to see their imperfections, leaving them open to your judgment or rejection. Reassurance is not going to help the narcissist at all; narcissists will display worse and worse behaviors in an attempt to see how far they can push someone before they leave.

- **Suffering from anxiety.**

Narcissists feel that something terrible is going to happen to them. They may show this anxiety by talking about the terrible things that they expect to happen, but narcissists hide their anxiety because they are afraid that it will make them vulnerable. Most narcissists are going to project this anxiety onto the people closest to them. They will call them mentally ill, selfish, or unsupportive. They do this so that they do not have to feel the anxiety. As they make you feel worse, they feel better. As your anxiety grows, theirs diminishes.

- **Being unable to feel guilt.**

The narcissist thinks that they are always right. They do not believe that the things that they do affect anyone besides themselves. Deep down, the narcissist may feel a lot of shame; they may understand that there is something wrong with them, even if they are unable to identify it. The narcissist feels ashamed of the fear that they feel, as well as their insecurities. The narcissist will try to hide this guilt in an attempt to hide their low self-esteem.

- **Being unable to communicate with others.**

While most people are in a relationship or working as part of a team, narcissists think about how their actions will affect the other person or persons. The narcissist never thinks about the other people in their lives. The narcissist will not give up something that they want to provide you with something that you want. They do not believe that you have your own feelings, therefore, they do not consider them.

A narcissist lacks boundaries. They tend to believe that everything and everyone belongs to them. If they are told "No", they become insulted. They behave like toddlers when they want something, going to extremes to get whatever it is they want. They will go as far as pouting, demanding, bugging you persistently about it, getting mad, and refusing to speak to you until they get what they want.

They are unable to empathize with other people. Because the narcissist is so self-absorbed, they rarely consider other people's feelings. A narcissist will rarely apologize for their behavior or feel remorse. They are completely focused on their own feelings and are blind to the way that they make other people feel.

When a narcissist feels that someone is doing something to upset them purposefully, they may react with anger. You may not be trying to upset the narcissist; however, in their mind, that is exactly what you are doing. For example, if the narcissist tries to tell you that the earth is flat and you show them all of the scientific proof that you can find, proving that the earth is round, they will feel that you have deliberately tried to make them look dumb.

They are also known to show off any of the qualities for which they think people will admire them. They want everyone to know how great they are doing at work; if they have done something nice, they will make sure to share it with the world. For example, if they were to give a homeless person a dollar, they would make it sound like they changed that person's life.

They believe that they excel at everything they try to do. Even when they may be having average or below average results, according to them, they are the best in the business.

A narcissistic person will exploit other people and manipulate them. They see people as a means to an end, not as another human that matters. They will do whatever it takes to get what they want from the people in their lives.

Chances are that you have met someone with some of these traits. Many people display at least one of these traits at one point or another in their lives. This is why it is so easy for narcissists to go undetected. It is very simple for a narcissist to come across as a caring person when you first meet them, and that is what makes them so dangerous. Once they pull you in, the red flags start to go up, but you are already emotionally invested. You tell yourself that they are having a bad day or that this is not really who they are. You start to make excuses for them, allowing them to continue to take advantage of you.

By learning about the traits of narcissists, you may be able to protect yourself from being taken advantage of down the road. You may also realize that you have a narcissist in your life already.

Chapter Three: Six Types of Narcissists You Should Know

Today we find that the word narcissist is thrown around fairly haphazardly to describe any person who is highly motivated, self-assured, or knows what they want out of life. The truth is that narcissism goes much deeper than that. Just because a person monopolizes the entire dinner conversation to talk about something that they recently accomplished does not make them a narcissist. A narcissistic person does not just feel that what they have done is important, but that *they* are important. Narcissism is a broad term, though. Within narcissism are several different types, each of them with their own traits and telling behaviors.

Toxic Narcissist - Have you ever known someone who seems to thrive off of causing drama in the lives of other people? Toxic narcissists spend their time causing drama for other people. If you do not meet their demands, they become angry and begin causing issues in your life. They do things like get you fired from a job, try to end your relationships with other people, and can even become physically abusive. (Never allow someone to cause you physical harm. Remove yourself from the situation, seek professional help, and contact local law enforcement to discuss your options.)

Narcissist with Psychopathic Tendencies - Only about 1% of the people in the world is considered psychopathic. However, there is a form of narcissism that comes with psychopathic tendencies. These people are very dangerous and should be avoided no matter what. They are often known for becoming very violent and having no remorse for their actions. When you think about this type of person, you should think about serial killers and other types of murderers as they are the ones that make up the majority of this category.

Closet Narcissists -The closet narcissist can hide their narcissistic traits, making it hard for anyone to identify them as a narcissist. The closet narcissist is still going to feel entitled; they are going to need validation and admiration, but they wear a mask, making themselves look selfless. Think about the person who is always posting on social media about all of the wonderful things they are doing for the world; volunteering at the animal shelter, feeding the homeless, or visiting the elderly. Most people do their good deeds quietly and privately, but the closet narcissist wants everyone to know about them. They want to be admired for all of the good things that they are doing. Most of the time, they don't even care about the people that they are helping; they are only helping so that they will get the attention that they desire.

Exhibitionist Narcissists - This type of narcissist does not care to hide that they are a narcissist. They will let everyone around them know; they are loud, and they are proud. They want to be in the spotlight all of the time, and when they are not, they become very upset. They tend to take advantage of other people seeing them as nothing more than steppingstones to get what they want in life.

Bully Narcissists - This type of narcissist is a self-absorbed bully; they are the people who have to put other people down to build themselves up. They are fixated on being number one and will threaten anyone who gets in their way. A regular bully is one who will bully a person for social or material gain; a bully narcissist will do it because it makes them feel better about who they are.

The Seducer- The seducer narcissist is very tricky. They start by making you feel great about who you are, to win your trust, admiration, or love. Once they have won you over, they will no longer be interested in you. Have you ever known someone who seemed to love the chase, but when they finally obtained the love and admiration of the person they were chasing, they were no longer interested? This is the seducer narcissist. They should be avoided because they can become abusive, and they feel no remorse for the pain that they are causing.

Most of us do not want to have any narcissists in our lives. They are dangerous and should be avoided. They can cause physical, mental, and emotional damage that can take years to repair. To avoid these types of people, you have to be able to identify them. Sadly, this can be a challenge even when you know what you are looking for. If you suspect that someone in your life is a narcissist, and they are displaying narcissistic behavior, the best thing that you can do is remove them from your life. No one has the right to be in your life if you do not want them to be. While the narcissist may react strongly and try to force their way back into your life, you must remain strong and stand your ground to stop them from causing any more harm.

Chapter Four: The Narcissist's Favorite Tools

If you have ever been in any type of relationship with a narcissist, you may have found yourself wondering how you ended up in the situation. You may not understand why you ended up trusting someone so selfish and manipulative.

Narcissists use a variety of tools to take advantage of you, to silence you, and to degrade you. The narcissist does not care if you are in a private or a public place; they will shame you whenever the opportunity arises. They do this to keep your self-esteem as low as possible, to make you feel as if you need their validation, which will keep you hoping that one day you will get their approval, one day you *will* be good enough. That day will never come. They may follow the shaming with "I was just joking" or another phrase like that, but their behavior is inexcusable.

> 1. When you first meet a narcissist, they can be extremely charming. They tend to sweep you off of your feet when you first meet them and may shower you with compliments. Soon the compliments stop, and the charming personality goes away. The narcissist has trapped you. When you meet a

person that is so charming that they seem to be too good to be true, accept that that is probably indeed the case.

2. The narcissist will always be the victim. If you have had a bad day, they will make sure that you know theirs was worse. No matter what is going on in your life, they are going to make sure that they can top it. Even though their goal is to victimize you, they are going to come across like a victim because it provides them with the attention that they crave. You may start wondering if your problems are really as big as you think they are or if you are just being overly dramatic. The narcissist wants you to feel this way. They want to make sure that you feel that their problems are much bigger than yours because it opens you up to being manipulated by them.

3. Gaslighting is one of the most well-known techniques that a narcissist will use. They do this to make the person question their own sanity. They may tell you that you imagined things that you know you remember, or that you dreamed them. This can cause you to feel as if you are losing your mind, which allows the narcissist to continue to victimize you.

4. A narcissist always wants to be at the top. They want to be in the spotlight all of the time, which means that when you have success in your life or when you achieve anything important, they want to downplay it. They want to make your successes seem less important than theirs. At first, they may complement your success a lot, even to the point that it seems too much. However, as their true colors start to show, they are going to start making you feel that the things you do are just not that good. They do this because it makes you work harder to impress them, which makes them look better and provides them with more attention.

5. Narcissists are known for projecting their shortcomings on to everyone else around them. They refuse to accept that they

are not perfect and refuse to take any responsibility for their own behavior unless, of course, they are getting praised for it. They are never going to focus on self-improvement because, in their eyes, they are perfect. Instead, they will simply project every one of their flaws and all of their bad behavior onto you. One example of this would be that when one spouse is having an affair, they accuse the other person of having one. They are unable to accept their own negative behavior, so they will project it onto their spouse. A lazy employee may claim that they have not been able to be successful at their job because their boss is ineffective. This allows them to maintain their view of themselves while escaping the truth about the situation.

6. Narcissists are great at starting arguments for which you have no idea how it began. You start a conversation with them, thinking that you are going to get to have a thoughtful conversation. Then they start using gaslighting, talking in circles, trying to confuse you and distract you from whatever it was that you were talking about. Disagreeing with them on even the most insignificant topic can lead to a huge argument. For example, if you tell them that the sky is blue instead of the shade of purple that they claim it is, not only is the idea of the sky being blue going to come under attack, but your entire life, every choice you have ever made, and every opinion that you have ever had will come under attack as well. Remember, they tend to thrive on causing drama, and every time that you disagree with them, you are providing them with an opening to cause drama. Don't feed into this. You don't have to prove your point if you know that you are right. Instead, accept that they are wrong and go on with your life. If you see that they are trying to start an argument, cut the conversation short and spend some time taking care of yourself instead of arguing with them.

---

7. Have you ever had someone misinterpret what you were saying to the point that it seemed absurd that they would come to that conclusion? This is what a narcissist will do. For example, let's say that you are talking to a narcissistic person discussing how you are unhappy with the way someone is treating you. They may respond by saying, "Oh yeah, because you're so perfect," or, "So suddenly I'm the bad guy!", when all you have done is express your feelings about how you are being treated. The narcissist does this to make you feel that you do not have the right to express your own feelings about their or anyone else's behavior. They will try to make you feel guilty about expressing your feelings. They may also claim to know what you are thinking.

Instead of listening to what is being said, they will jump to conclusions about the situation and put words in your mouth. They will say things like, "So you think that I am a bad friend," or, "If you don't want me around, just let me know, and I'll go." This is their preemptive defense. By behaving this way, they make you feel sorry for them, and they ensure that you will not voice your opinion or your feelings in the future. If you react to what they are saying, it is only going to feed into the argument. Instead, simply tell them that you never said that and walk away from the conversation. You are going to show them that you will not be controlled and that you have boundaries that they cannot cross.

1. Moving the goalpost is a technique that many narcissists will use to ensure that they can express how dissatisfied with you they are. They may tell you that they expect one thing, but when you do it, they will say they expected something different. They will criticize everything you do, setting impossible standards and nitpicking instead of helping you to improve. Let's say that you have lost 20 pounds and you are proud of your success. The narcissist will ask why you have not lost 30. If you get a raise at work, they will ask why it was not more. They do not want you to be proud of any of

your accomplishments, so they will make it seem as if you have fallen short. They may even bring up something that has nothing to do with what you were talking about. For example, if you tell them that you got a raise, they may say, "Well, now you can start paying attention to your appearance." They do this to make sure that you are always striving for their approval. When they continually raise their expectations of you, they ensure that you never feel that you are quite good enough for them.

2. Another technique that a narcissist will use is to change the subject to ensure they are not held accountable for their actions. A narcissist does not want to allow anyone to hold them accountable for anything. When they notice that you are starting to hold them accountable, they will change the subject to make themselves look like the victim. They will talk about how they were wronged growing up, how everyone mistreats them, or even go as far as bringing up something that you did years ago that upset them. When this is done, the discussion is derailed, and you do not get to say what you wanted to say. Do not allow them to derail you. If you notice that they are trying to change the subject, switch it back. Become a broken record redirecting the conversation. You can say, "That is not what I was talking about; let's try to focus on this issue." If they refuse, end the conversation and spend your time doing something more productive. There is no point in wasting your time trying to have a conversation with them when they just want to keep changing the subject.

3. A narcissist will use threats when they feel that their sense of superiority is being challenged. They may make very unreasonable demands of you while making sure that you know that you are not living up to their expectations. Instead of talking through a disagreement or behaving maturely, they will try to make you afraid of any consequences that could happen as a result of you disagreeing with them. They

threaten their victims, either covertly or overtly. This should be a red flag, and it should tell you that they will not compromise. These threats should be taken seriously. If you are ever threatened, make sure that the threat is documented and report it to the police immediately.

4. When their sense of superiority is threatened, the narcissist will blow things out of proportion. In their mind, they can't be wrong, and anyone that would suggest otherwise is a threat. When their sense of superiority is threatened, it could result in narcissistic rage. This is not due to their low self-esteem but instead from their extremely high sense of entitlement. Name-calling is a form of narcissistic rage. They use this technique when they are unable to come up with a different way to manipulate you. It allows them to put you down quickly, insult you, and make them feel better about who they are. Instead of focusing on what you are saying, replying to your comments with facts, they will start calling you names in an attempt to make you appear less credible or intelligent. If name-calling begins, end the conversation right away. Do not tolerate anyone calling you names. Remember that you should not take these names to heart, either. They do not represent who you are but who the narcissist is.

5. Further notes on gaslighting (a technique that narcissists use to make their victim question their own sanity): to ensure that the narcissist is not able to use gaslighting on you, you will have to trust your own memories. If you are afraid that you are going to forget details about what happened, write it down. Keep a journal. Write down the date, the time, exactly what happened and what was said. When you bring this with you to any conversation, they are going to be faced with facts, and you will be able to ensure that you are not relying solely on your memory. When you write things down, you are going to be able to trust that it happened exactly the way that you remember it happening.

6. While many narcissists are very smart, the majority of them are not masterminds; they simply want you to believe that they are. Most narcissists will not take the time to do any research. They will not try to understand any other perspectives but their own. Instead, they are going to generalize everything and make blanket statements that will invalidate any experiences that do not fit into their stereotypes. For example, if there was a news report about a well-known figure making a rape accusation, they may remind you that many rape allegations are false. They may try to make it seem that while falsely reported rape allegations do happen on rare occasions, the majority of rapes are falsely reported.

Or they may make a blanket statement about you, such as, "You are always complaining," or "You always do that." Instead of taking the time to address the specific issue that has upset you, they generalize. The chances are that you might complain now and then, but you don't *always* complain. The chances are higher that the narcissist spends the majority of *their* time complaining and being cruel.

1. A narcissistic person will make sure that you associate memories that should be happy, such as holidays or vacations, with abuse, disrespect, or frustration. They are going to try to ruin every holiday by making it all about them and can even isolate you from the people that you love. They do this to make sure that they are the center of attention. Their goal is to ensure that you are focusing all of your attention on them all of the time. If you can reach your goals and find happiness without depending on them, it threatens their role in your life.

2. When a narcissist is unable to control the way that you feel about yourself, they will take steps to control the way that other people feel about you. They will make it look as if you are the toxic one in the relationship, and they are the victim. They will do whatever they need to destroy your reputation,

ensuring that you have no one to turn to if you decide to cut ties with them. If you are still able to separate yourself from them, they may end up stalking you and claim that they are trying to let everyone know the truth about who you really are.

Not only will a narcissist shame you to your face, but they will gossip about you when you are not around. They will go as far as making up stories about you and claiming to be the victim of the abuse that they are heaping on you.

If this is happening to you, you need to make sure that you are mindful of the way that you react to the narcissist. Always focus on sticking to the facts whenever you have to interact with them. This is especially important if you were married to a narcissist and are going through a divorce. Make sure that you have documentation of any type of harassment. Print out the private messages that they have sent you. Contact law enforcement, when necessary to document the abuse. If you do have to speak to the narcissist, make sure that your lawyer is present.

> 1. The narcissist is known for belittling the victim. Instead of using sarcasm for fun, they use it to manipulate you. If you say anything about their sarcasm, they may tell you that you are just too sensitive. They tend to forget that they act like a two-year-old whenever they receive negative feedback from anyone. When you are faced with this type of abuse, you will begin questioning your feelings every time you think about voicing your own opinions or talking about your feelings. Suddenly you stop talking about the way that the narcissist makes you feel, and they no longer have to work to keep you silent.

If you find that someone is speaking to you in a demeaning way, speak up. Be firm when you let them know that you are not going to be spoken to like a child and that you are not going to be silent to make them feel better about who they are.

These are just a few of the techniques that narcissists use to control and manipulate their victims. An entire book could be written on this subject alone. Therefore, you need to know what your boundaries are. What type of behavior are you willing to accept, and what type of behavior is unacceptable in any relationship that you are in? Once you know what you will not accept, you will be able to recognize manipulation techniques more easily.

Chapter Five: How Narcissists Choose Their Victims

Have you ever met someone that you felt an instant connection to only to find out that all they wanted to do was manipulate you? Have you ever shared your secrets with someone only to find out that they purposefully collected the information to use it against you later? This is usually how things play out when we meet narcissists.

When you are a compassionate, caring, and trusting person, you want to believe that other people are the same. We all want to believe that people are good. Sadly, this is not always the case. Sometimes we come across people in our lives who only want us in their lives for their own selfish gains.

These people are emotional parasites. They target you, and they take advantage of you. Deep down, you know that something is off in the relationship, but because the narcissist is so good at playing the victim, you feel as if you have to stick it out. After all, everyone else in their life has abandoned them.

Once you have been targeted by a narcissist, you may find yourself wondering why they chose you. You may feel that you are to blame somehow for the way that they have treated you. The truth is that a narcissist's behavior is not your fault. You have done nothing to deserve the treatment that you have received. Narcissists are predators seeking out people on whom they can feed.

When you look back at the relationship, you may realize that you were not the one that started it up; it was the narcissist that initiated it. Realizing that *they* chose *you* may make you wonder, "Why you?" – what was it about you that screamed out to them that they could take advantage of you? There are many things that a narcissist will look for in a victim, including:

- There is something that you have that the narcissist wants; a specific lifestyle, money, power, or a position.
- You are a caregiver or someone who has a deep desire to help other people. If this sounds like you be very careful, because you are a beacon to narcissists, one of their favorite types of victims.
- You are empathetic. If you are an empath, you are the prime candidate for a narcissist.
- You grew up in a dysfunctional home. If you grew up in an abusive environment, it could make it harder for you to identify abuse in the early stages. It can also make it very hard for you to set boundaries. The narcissist will do whatever it takes to take advantage of this weakness to ensure that you are left completely dependent upon them.
- You are desperate to find someone to love, or you feel lonely. When you feel lonely or desperate to love, you are going to lower your standards. You just want someone there to fill the void. The narcissist will jump right into position, not to love you but to victimize you.
- You are okay with accepting blame even when you didn't do anything. If you are the type of person who is willing to accept blame for things that go wrong in your relationships, even when you are not at fault, you will be the perfect victim

for a narcissist. They love to place the blame on other people even when it is obvious that they are in the wrong.

• You don't like confrontation and try to avoid conflict at all costs. Narcissists do not want to be in a relationship with someone that is going to confront them about their behavior. Instead, they will seek out someone who avoids conflict because that shows them that they will always be able to take control of any situation in that relationship. They will always get their way.

Before a narcissist chooses their victim, they will test the person. The narcissist will use different techniques to determine if they are going to be able to victimize the person in whom they are interested.

One of the techniques that a narcissist will use is to suggest that you change something about who you are. They may suggest that you change the type of clothes that you wear, the makeup that you wear, your hair, your personality, or your weight. You may be surprised at the suggestion; when you first meet someone and they ask you to change something, such as your hair color or your personality, red flags should go up. Having someone tell you right after meeting you that you need to relax more and let your guard down should scream "narcissist" to you. This is one of the first signs that you are entering a relationship with a narcissist.

When you first meet someone, you do not start telling them all of the things they need to change about themselves. You would never do this to someone, so do not allow anyone to do it to you. Many people fall into this trap, hoping that the relationship has long-term potential when instead, the narcissist just wants to see if you will do what they tell you.

A narcissist will tell you that they are going to call you or come over at a certain time or on a certain day, and then they just don't. You may find yourself completely confused as the days pass and you do not hear from them, only to find them calling or showing up several days later as if nothing happened. They have been out enjoying life and having a blast while you have been at home waiting on them to call you or come over and trying to understand why they haven't.

The narcissist will do this to determine how not calling or coming over has affected you. They are doing this on purpose, even if they have some amazing excuse. I can assure you that this was a test. They may tell you that they had to go out of town suddenly or that they completely forgot to call you. That is not the truth. This test was planned ahead of time to determine how you would react.

Of course, that is not to say that every time this happens you are dealing with a narcissist. If you are in a relationship with someone and this happens one time, the chances are something really did interfere with their plans. If it happens again, though, it is not a mistake. If it happens a second time, you need to recognize that you are dealing with a narcissist. Do not allow them to see that their not calling has bothered you. When they find out that they are not able to affect you, they will go looking for a different victim.

Have you ever met a person who tried to get you to trust them right away? You should be very alert if this happens to you. A person who tells you right after they have met you that you can trust them and that they will not hurt you is likely a narcissist.

This is not to say that you should be on guard 24 hours per day, seven days a week, because there are some great people out in the world. What you do need to be aware of is that trustworthy people do not have to tell someone that they are trustworthy. They are never going to try to convince you to trust them, and they will never try to discuss sensitive topics when they first meet you.

Most of us know that a healthy relationship will progress naturally. In the beginning, you don't want to trust too much, especially if you are still healing from previous relationships. Instead of rushing into things quickly, allow them to progress naturally. One of the biggest mistakes that people make is creating instant relationships with someone they just met. It may seem flattering when someone you just met wants to start an instant relationship, but it should be a red flag.

You may feel excited about all of the attention that you are getting from the narcissist, but deep down, you know that boundaries are being crossed. The narcissist will start violating boundaries as soon as they meet you. They want to find someone that has weak boundaries or no boundaries at all because they know that they are going to be able to enter a relationship with this person and get exactly what they want without having to do anything in return.

Honest people who are trusting and compassionate are the perfect target for a narcissist who is going to start testing boundaries right away. If you do not make your boundaries clear or you don't have any, you will become a target. Many people have a hard time setting boundaries within their relationships. They do not want to cause conflict, nor do they want to be seen as confrontational, which is exactly what a narcissist will look for.

You don't have to have strong boundaries with those that you love; however, when it comes to a person that you have just met, it is important to establish those boundaries right away. This is important because if at some point, you get into a relationship with that person, it is almost impossible to implement boundaries. When you establish them from the start, they are already there.

One thing that you need to remember is that if you have suffered any trauma in your childhood, you can become a target for narcissists. Remind yourself that you are no longer that helpless child. You are a strong and capable adult that can build boundaries and ensure that they are not violated.

Finally, when a narcissist is testing someone to determine if they are going to be their next victim, they will start sharing stories about how bad their childhood was or how terribly their exes treated them. They do this to make you feel sorry for them. Remember when we talked about how the narcissist always plays the victim? This is part of that technique.

The conversation can begin with them asking questions about your childhood or past relationships, but it will end with them oversharing things that have happened to them in the past. It is important to remember that these events may have occurred, but they may have not. The narcissist is not going to have a problem telling you that they were abused, even when they were not, to get you to feel sorry for them so they can take advantage of you.

There is one thing that all of these tests have in common, and it is that they take place right after you have met the narcissist. If you find that someone is oversharing, wanting to know far too much about you too quickly, or is wanting to jump into a very serious relationship very quickly, red flags should go up.

Walking away from a narcissist can be scary at first, but all of the pain that they have made you feel does go away. Seeking professional help when ending a relationship with a narcissist can help you to overcome the damage that they have caused. You can get your life back, though. You can be empowered and independent once again.

Chapter Six: Match Made in Hell: Narcissists and Empaths

An empath is a person that is able to tune into the emotions of those around them. They can tune into the emotions of both people and animals. The empath not only can understand how someone is feeling but many times they will take those emotions into themselves, feeling them as if they were their own.

Empaths are highly sensitive to those around them and may find themselves overwhelmed with emotion when they are in a crowd. They do not only pick up on the emotions of the people that they are talking to, but the emotions of everyone around them.

The trait that most puts an empath in danger around a narcissist is that they are unable to see a person who is hurting, either emotionally or physically, without having the desire to help them. When they see a person in need, they are not able to turn their backs on them. It does not matter how busy the empath is, or how rushed; they will do whatever they can to help someone. This is what makes them so vulnerable.

The empath is the exact opposite of a narcissist, and as you know, opposites tend to attract. Empaths are extremely understanding and filled with compassion, while the narcissist needs someone who is going to praise them constantly. The empath will forgive the narcissist no matter what they do, which will result in the empath being degraded and used while the narcissist thrives in the relationship.

Narcissists will seek out empaths because they know that the empath is going to fulfill every selfish need that they have. The empath is very attracted to the narcissist because they are caregivers, exactly what the narcissist needs.

When a narcissist sees an empath, they see someone who is caring, loving, devoted, and who will bend over backward to make them happy. When the narcissist sets their eyes on a target, they will put up a false front, pretending that they are a loving and compassionate person; as the empath enters the relationship, they are only going to see all of the good qualities of the narcissist, even though the qualities are fake. Of course, the narcissist can only fake it for so long; they will begin pointing out the empath's flaws, while the empath believes that they can help fix the narcissist. The empath's natural instinct tells them that as long as they are compassionate enough, they will be able to heal the narcissist.

They find themselves thinking the relationship would grow fruitful if they only listened more, gave more, tried harder, and on and on. This type of mindset is never going to work when you are in a relationship with a narcissist. Yet the empath is unable to give up on someone; it hurts them to think that they cannot help the person that they love. So, they try harder.

The empath is going to work hard to create harmony within the relationship while the narcissist is going to focus on creating chaos and drama, thereby manipulating the empath. A narcissist will manipulate the empath by making them believe that there is some hope of change. They will provide the empath with little complements or even small acts of kindness which make the empath believe that they have done something right, and if they continue, things will change. Empaths are long-suffering; they understand that we are all just humans and don't expect anyone to be perfect. A narcissist can manipulate an empath by simply telling them, "I'm not perfect. I am trying to change." While the narcissist may admit fault, they do not believe that they are faulty, and they have no intention of making any changes. This is just another technique that they use to manipulate the empath. The empath wants to provide support. They want to help the narcissist grow and become a better person. In the end, the narcissist is just exploiting them.

An empath can look at themselves and recognize their own faults. The narcissist can take advantage of this while forming the trauma bond. The empath will start focusing on the things that they need to change to make the relationship better. The narcissist can point out all of the empath's flaws, and the empath accepts what they are being told.

It can be very difficult for an empath to recognize that they are in a relationship with a narcissist. As an empath, you have to be very careful about the people with whom you form relationships. You have to make sure that you are trying to get them to grow in life but not doing all of the work on your own. You have to take a step back and look at the bigger picture. What steps are *they* taking to make things better?

It is also important to put up boundaries. We talked a little bit about boundaries in the last chapter, but for an empath, boundaries are extremely important. Empaths tend to feel like boundaries are harsh. They have a hard time saying "No" to people. However, that one word can protect an empath from being exploited.

You don't have to become hard-hearted to protect yourself from a narcissist. What you do have to do is accept that not every person is meant to be in your life. You are going to come across people all of the time that are not healthy for you to be in a relationship with, and that is perfectly okay.

If you are an empath and you are in a relationship with a narcissist, you can change the situation by empowering yourself. At first, you are going to notice that the narcissist will push back. They do this because they recognize that the balance of power is starting to shift, and it makes them feel threatened. As an empath, you will need to focus on allowing other people to experience their own emotions and not taking them upon yourself. As the balance of power begins to shift, the narcissist is going to start noticing that you still have a voice. This may make them push back even harder, or they may give up and find another victim.

Understandably, this could be frightening. When you love someone, you want to make them happy. You want to do things for them, and you do not want to do something that is going to make them leave. However, when you are in a relationship with a narcissist, you have to understand that they do not feel the same way about you. You are nothing more than a means to an end for them. You provide them with what they want, and if you are not going to do that any longer, they are going to find someone else to exploit.

We have to be aware that there is a difference between empowering yourself and trying to force the narcissist to change. The narcissist will never change. You, however, can. A narcissist can make you feel as if you will not be able to live without them. They may make you feel that you need them to take care of you and to make decisions for you. They use gaslighting to make you feel as if you are not capable of making decisions on your own. They will attack your self-esteem, putting you down as much as possible in hopes of making you comply with their demands.

If you are in a relationship with a narcissist, you need to make sure that you do not argue with them or try to defend yourself. Simply tell them that you disagree and leave the conversation. Allow the narcissist to deal with their emotions on their own. I know that this can be hard for you, but it is the best way for you to start taking control back from the narcissist.

Chapter Seven: 12 Phrases Narcissists Use (and What to Say Back)

If you have ever been in a relationship with a narcissist - or any type of toxic person for that matter - you probably have a bit of an understanding as to how they use language to manipulate you. They use specific phrases every day that would be used in a completely different text if they were not a narcissist.

Studies have shown that a narcissist enjoys manipulating kindhearted people; they view it as a kind of sport. They believe that they are superior. By manipulating you, they are building on this belief even when all of the evidence points otherwise.

They will use conversations as a way to bring you down or terrorize you. They will cause you to be so afraid to disagree with what they say that you will just give up and agree with them. To understand what a narcissist really means when they are talking to us, we have to decode their language. These phrases below are the most commonly used by narcissists followed by what the narcissist really means.

1. **"I love you."** – I love being able to control you, use you, and own you. I love that I can sweet-talk you, make you

believe that I care about you, and toss you to the side as I please. I love that when I flatter you, I can get whatever it is that I want. I love that you have opened up to me even though you were mistreated in the past. I love that I have been able to get you to trust me. I love knowing that I can pull the rug out from under you whenever I want, and watch you crumble.

2. "I'm sorry."– I am not sorry. I want this conversation to end so that I can continue enjoying taking advantage of you. I do not care that you were hurt by what I did. I am only sorry that I was caught. I do not like that you are calling me out and trying to hold me accountable for my actions. I do not like dealing with your emotions. They are not valid as far as I am concerned because they interfere with me getting what I want. I do not care how you feel.

3. "You are overreacting" *or* **"too sensitive."** – While you may be having a perfectly normal reaction to all of the abuse that I have put you through, I do not like that you are starting to recognize what is going on. I am going to gaslight you to ensure that you continue to second-guess yourself. I need to make sure that you know that your emotions are invalid to ensure that you do not try to stand up to me. I know that if you do not trust yourself, you are going to continue to deny the abuse that I am putting you through. You will rationalize my behavior, blaming yourself for it. While you are busy blaming yourself, you are going to be working very hard to keep me happy. I get all of the benefits without any of the consequences.

4. "You are going crazy." – I know that you are not crazy, but I love provoking you and making you think that you are losing your mind. By pointing my finger and saying that you are the crazy one, I can make sure that the focus is taken off of me and put back onto you. It doesn't matter anyway. I have ensured that no one is going to believe anything that you have to say. They already know how unstable you are. I can make them believe anything about you.

5. "My ex is crazy." – My ex really is not crazy, and if he/she is crazy, it is because I made them that way. I had so much fun, torturing, provoking, and agitating them. I was always able to get a reaction out of them, which I used against them to prove to everyone just how crazy they were. Don't worry; I'll tell everyone how crazy you are as well.

6. "They are just a friend." – I keep him or her around in case you start to bore me. If I ever get tired of you or if you begin to bore me, they could be your replacement. They are already taking your place when I don't feel like being around you. If you complain about what I am doing, I am going to make sure that everyone believes you are the one that is trying to control me. I will make sure that you seem like the abusive one.

7. "Stop being so jealous." – I love making you jealous. I love that you are willing to compete with other people for my attention. It makes me feel so powerful, knowing that I can make you jealous so easily. I can create insecurities within you simply by flirting with another person. The more insecure you feel, the more powerful I feel. Everything that you believe is going on really is, but there is nothing that you can do about it. I am entitled to do whatever I want with whoever I want.

8. "Your trust issues are not my fault." – Sure, I know that you should not trust me. I know that I am going to go behind your back whenever I want and do whatever I want, but I'm not going to admit that to you. It would probably be best if you trusted your instincts and got away from me as quickly as possible, but then I wouldn't be having any fun. I enjoy seeing you question your instincts.

9. "It's not always about you." – It's actually never about you. In fact, it is always about me. If you ever decide to start focusing on what you want or need, I will make sure that you feel like the most self-centered person on the planet. I am going to make sure that you feel guilty for even considering taking care of your own needs. I have no desire to fulfill your needs; I couldn't do it if I wanted to. But I don't want to. The focus needs to be on what is important, and that is me.

10. "Can we still be friends?" – I want to keep you around in case I need to manipulate you in the future. I hate to see someone that I worked so hard to train just disappear. I like keeping track of all of my exes. That way, whenever I need some extra reassurance, they are right there for me to start manipulating all over again. Staying friends just makes it easier for me to keep a hold on you. This way, you will never truly be free of me.

11. "No one will ever believe you." – I have made sure that you are completely isolated and have no one to turn to for support. I have destroyed your reputation, making sure that everyone believes every lie that I have ever told about the person that you are. I have made sure that everyone knows that I am the victim in this relationship. If you go looking for help, not one person will believe what you tell them, and they are all still going to think that I am amazing.

12. "You're never going to find another person like me." – It will probably be a really good thing if you never find another person like me. There are people out there who are willing to treat you much better than I ever have. I don't want you to find out that they are out there, though. If you discover your worth, you could leave, and then I have to start all over with another victim. I would rather you just continue trying to make me happy.

Knowing the most common phrases that narcissists use and what they really mean is only half of the battle; it is also important for you to know how to react to what the narcissist is saying. When you know ahead of time how you are going to react to what the narcissist in your life says, you will be able to remain calm and in control. This is going to infuriate them because they are going to begin to see that they do not have control over you any longer. They will recognize that you are starting to take control back from them.

One of the biggest mistakes that people make when they come face to face with a narcissist is trying to get the narcissist to see the logic. You cannot use logic when a narcissist wants to start an argument. They actually enjoy it when you do this because it allows them to use their techniques to make you feel poorly about your views, thoughts, and feelings. Knowing how to respond to them will ensure that you can stop allowing them to take control of these situations.

To do this, you are going to need a few strategies of your own that will help you to stay grounded when the narcissist tries to attack you verbally. These strategies allow you to maintain control of your own emotions even when the narcissist is trying to make you lose control. These five statements can be used whenever you feel that the narcissist is trying to take control from you.

> 1. **"Thank you for telling me how you feel."** You can use this phrase whenever you are having a conversation with a narcissist, and they are trying to blame-shift. This shows them that while you have heard what they have said, you are not going to allow it to affect you emotionally. After you have made this statement, you will simply go back to focusing on whatever your point was before they started trying to blame you for the situation.

For example:

> Stacy and Todd had been dating for a few months. Stacy needed to talk to Todd about how he flirted with other women when the

two of them would go out on dates. When Stacy sat down to have a conversation with Todd, he became angry.

"You're too jealous," his voice boomed as he tried to make her feel bad for her own feelings.

"Thank you for letting me know how you feel," Stacy calmly replied, "I do not appreciate the way that you behave toward other women when we are out together. I deserve more respect than what you are giving me, and your behavior is unacceptable."

As you can see, Stacy did not become defensive as Todd had hoped. Instead, she used her strategy to remain calm and focus on the issue at hand. She refused to allow Todd to control her as he tried to shift the blame to her.

2. **"I wanted you to know how I feel."** We are all tempted to try and ensure that the narcissist knows how we feel; we hope that if they start to understand how they make us feel, they will change their behavior. But they are not going to understand how you feel, nor are they going to care. They know that you want them to understand the damage that they are doing, but as a narcissist, they are going to focus on ensuring you only get the opposite of what you are asking. However, we all need to be able to express ourselves and our feelings. Saying, "I wanted you to know how I feel" allows you to express yourself while maintaining emotional control. Once you have made this statement, you will end the conversation right there.

3. **"Thank you for expressing your opinion."** You can use this phrase when the narcissist goes on and on about a specific thing or when it is obvious that they are just trying to get a reaction out of you. Using this phrase allows the narcissist to express their "feelings" as we all should be able to do, but it also shows them that no matter what their opinions are, you are not going to lose control of your

emotions. When you use this phrase, you are not telling them that you agree with their opinion or telling them that your opinion is wrong. Instead, you are ensuring that you do not feel the desire to have the same opinions as the narcissist. You are never going to have the same opinions as them, no matter how much they try to force you to do so.

4. **"I'm sorry that you feel like that."** You can use this when the narcissist starts using name-calling or tries putting you down.

For example:

Todd knew that he was losing control of Stacy. She had been going out and making new friends, doing things on her own, and he could feel his grip slipping.

"You are the reason that we have so many problems in this relationship," he towered over Stacy as he looked down at her with anger, "If it wasn't for you, we would all be much happier."

"I'm sorry that you feel like that," Stacy calmly replied. She knew that she no longer needed his approval.

You see, Stacy was starting to understand that Todd would do anything to maintain control of the situation. He was trying to convince her that if she tried harder to make him happy, the relationship would be better. Stacy knew that this was just one of the many techniques that Todd used as a narcissist.

When you respond this way to a narcissist's insults, you are not allowing them to affect you. Instead, you recognize that they are trying to insult you, but you also understand that it is what they think, it has nothing to do with who you truly are.

5. **"We have two different opinions on the matter."**

Agreeing that the two of you disagree is going to stop the narcissist from being able to start an argument. This phrase is going to shock the narcissist because they have spent a lot of time training you, making sure that they can make you agree with anything that they say. You may not have even realized up until this point that you have agreed with everything that the narcissist says; you may have found yourself overexplaining your views or opinions, and the reason for this is because deep down, you feel like you need them to approve of what you think. When they don't approve, you simply change your opinions.

Using these phrases allows you to remain calm and think more clearly. When you allow a narcissist to upset you emotionally, you are not able to think clearly about the situation. The narcissist is counting on this happening because they know that if they can keep you from thinking clearly, they will be able to maintain control over you.

A strange thing happens when a narcissist can get you emotionally frustrated. The more frustrated you become, the calmer the narcissist will become. This can make you feel as if you are losing your sanity. On the other hand, when you use these phrases, what you are going to find is that the calmer you are, the more frustrated the narcissist is going to become.

None of these phrases are used to calm the narcissist or make them happy with the way that things are going. These phrases are going to help make you happy, and help you take control of your life away from the narcissist so that you can live your best life.

You should be prepared for the way that the narcissist is going to react when you use these phrases. When you use these phrases, the narcissist is going to realize that they are no longer able to project who they are onto you. This is going to cause them a lot of distress, and they are going to push back.

When you are talking to a narcissist, whether you are in a relationship with them or not, you are going to want to make sure that you let them know that they do not scare you. One of the most common techniques that a narcissist will use is to intimidate their victim. They try to bully you into getting you to do what they want.

Ask yourself, "What's the worse that they can do?" Chances are you are going to realize that their worst is much better than what you have been dealing with.

Example:

Todd was at his wit's end. He knew he had to get control of Stacy, but so far, he had been unable to do so. What had suddenly given her this power to stand against him? He knew what she was afraid, of and he knew exactly what he was going to do.

"I came to a decision," Todd walked into the kitchen, returning home from work.

Stacy turned around, looking at him as dinner simmered on the stovetop.

"Really," Stacy raised an eyebrow, wondering what technique he was going to try next.

"I'm going to give it one week," Todd replied, his chest puffed out, "If things don't change, then I'm gone."

Stacy had read about threats. She thought for a moment. What was the worst that could happen? He would leave, find a new victim, and she would be left to start healing from all of the abuse.

"Hmm," Stacy nodded her head as she turned back to the stove.

"What does that mean," Todd's voice was getting louder. Why was she not begging him for a second chance? Why wasn't she upset with his threats?

"I guess if that is what you want, it's your decision to make." Stacy stirred the food, ensuring that it did not burn. She could feel the anger building in Todd as he stood behind her. She refused to react. Sure, she loved him. It broke her heart when she realized that she was nothing more than another victim to him. But she had decided that she was going to be happy in life and she was not going to allow him to take her happiness away from her.

Stacy truly would be better off if Todd would follow through with his threats. Most of the time, this never happens, at least until the narcissist realizes that they have lost all control. The narcissist is not one to give up, though. The majority of the time, it is the victim that must stand strong and end the relationship.

One thing that I do have to mention about threats is that if they are threats of violence or if the narcissist threatens your life, you need to contact the authorities and get help right away. Far too often, people do not take these threats seriously until the narcissist follows through with them. These narcissists are usually narcissistic with psychotic tendencies.

You can use logic when talking to a narcissist, to a point. You are not going to be able to use logic to get them to change their mind about something but using logic to question what they are saying works great.

Example:

Stacy and Todd sat down at the dinner table. Stacy loved to cook and had made a beautiful dinner for the two of them to share. She smiled at her handiwork as she looked down at her plate.

"You know, maybe if you didn't eat so much, you could lose a little weight, and I'd be more attracted to you." Todd was giving it another go. He was going to try his best to maintain control of her.

"You do know that I weigh 105 pounds, which is well within my healthy weight zone?" Stacy smiled as she stuffed a huge forkful of food into her mouth.

What was Todd going to say?

"Well, I think you look fat." he mumbled, scowling at her.

"I'm sorry you feel that way." Stacy replied as she continued to enjoy her meal.

Stacy was able to remain calm as she used logic to block Todd's attacks. He intended to cause her pain, but Stacy made sure that it did not happen. Even if she had not known that Todd wanted to hurt her, knowing that she was at a healthy weight for her height allowed her to block his attack that many people would have been deeply hurt by. Many times, the narcissist will simply change the subject when the victim responds logically. Remember, you cannot respond logically if you cannot think clearly, and you cannot think clearly if you allow the narcissist to get you worked up emotionally.

You must never allow a narcissist to make a single decision for you. Even something as small as eating a specific meal that they suggest is going to give them a sense of control. Instead, simply say, "Actually, I want this…" while remaining calm. Do what you said you wanted to do and not what the narcissist suggested for you to do.

On the same note, you should never allow a narcissist to order you around. You are not the hired help, and you should not be treated as such. If you find that the narcissist in your life is barking orders at you instead of asking, you could say something like, "Sure, I'd love to if you asked me nicely." When you do this, it is going to not only shock the narcissist, but it is going to force them to change their behavior. Whenever the narcissist starts making demands, simply repeat the phrase and let them know that it is not going to happen unless they learn how to ask politely. If they demand something of you that you do not want to do, simply tell them NO.

Learning how to say no without feeling the need to explain yourself is going to cause the narcissist a lot of distress. Narcissists do not want anyone to tell them no, but when someone does, they expect a really good explanation for it. You, however, do not owe them an explanation when you say no. You shouldn't even try to provide them with one because they usually try to twist what you have said around so that you feel bad. Don't allow them the opportunity to do this.

While nothing is going to stop the narcissist's behavior, using the techniques that you have learned in this chapter are going to allow you to block their behavior from affecting you. What is more important is that they are going to see that you are not going to allow them to victimize you, and while that will drive them crazy, they will usually become bored and go looking for a new victim.

Chapter Eight: Dealing with a Narcissist

Sometimes we have narcissists in our lives that we can walk away from very easily. Sometimes it can be difficult or almost impossible to walk away. Sometimes the narcissist in our lives is a coworker or a family member. Sometimes they are our parents.

While you may not always be able to walk away from every narcissist in your life, you can learn how to deal with a narcissist to bring peace back into your life.

Not all narcissists are abusive. However, if you are in an abusive relationship with a narcissist, these techniques may not work. Instead of trying to deal with the narcissist, you need to start trying to focus on what it is that makes you stay. Why do you continue to subject yourself to the abuse at the hands of the narcissist? It does not matter if it is mental, emotional, or physical, abuse of any kind is abuse, and you do not have to accept being treated that way. Please alert the authorities to what is going on and seek professional help so that you can deal with the damage that has been done. Remember, the abuse that the narcissist has inflicted upon you is not your fault. They are responsible for their actions, and nothing that you could do or say would make it okay for anyone to abuse you.

Before we get into learning how to deal with a narcissist, we have to first start by talking about denial. We can all spot denial when we see it. We see people all the time living in denial, not wanting to face the truth. A narcissist will be in denial about being a narcissist. How far in denial they are at the time will affect how well the techniques that we are going to talk about work. If the narcissist is deep in denial, these techniques may not work as well as they would if there was only a bit of denial.

How can you determine this?

Can the narcissist admit that there is a problem? Something as simple as admitting that their life is not what they expected it to be can provide you with some hope. Many people do not believe that a narcissist can admit that there is a problem, but the truth is that many of them have sought out therapy of some sort to help them understand what is going on. These are vulnerable narcissists, and you can learn how to deal with them.

When you are dealing with a narcissist, you have to be aware of the manipulation. We already know that narcissists are great manipulators, which means that they can convince you that they are changing, that they are interested in changing, or that they know there is a problem... but only if they think that they are going to benefit from doing so. Of course, not all narcissists will take things this far. However, those that are willing to are very dangerous because they can make you believe that they are willing to change and go through all of the motions, completely deceiving you.

You should also determine if they are willing to change. Just because you have a deep desire for them to change does not mean that they have that same desire. The best option would be for them to see a therapist. Are they willing to take that step to change? Most people who want to change are willing to do whatever it takes to see that change come to pass in their lives. Are they?

It is also important for you to take a good look at yourself. Are you extremely angry with them? The narcissist has probably spent a lot of time putting you down or name-calling. They may have openly talked about how attractive they find other people in their lives. It is possible that if you are in a relationship with a narcissist that they have cheated on you. When we are faced with all of this, our natural instinct is to make sure that we are protected from any damage that they would do. Many of us end up wearing full armor whenever we are around that person to ensure that no matter what they say, we do not suffer pain.

Anyone that has had to deal with narcissists in their lives would take measures to protect themselves, and that is completely understandable. The problem with this full suit of armor is that it can stop the narcissist in our lives from seeing the damage that they are doing. They are unable to see how sad you are, that they are causing fear, or that you love them. You have completely detached from them and the situation as a means of protecting yourself.

Can you remove some of that armor and allow the narcissist to know how you feel? If they say something hurtful or demeaning, calmly let them know exactly what they have done and how it made you feel. Start with a positive, "You mean so much to me." Then tell them how you are feeling, "When you say things to me like that, it makes me feel worthless and that you do not care about me at all."

Studies have shown that when people in a relationship learn to express themselves this way, their relationship is repaired far more often than it fails, and it is actually stronger than ever before.

Anger is not the only thing that you have to check, but you also need to understand how you are responding to the narcissist. Are you responding with silence? It is so easy for us to become angered by condescending remarks that a narcissist makes; however, once they have broken you down, their remarks often lead you to shutting down. How often are you shutting down? You may find that you are spending hours on end without saying a single word. If you want things to get better, you are going to have to learn how to speak up. Find your voice.

When a person withdraws into silence, they are using their coping skills to deal with the sadness or fear that the other person has caused them; this is a natural impulse. Sometimes, though, we have to learn how to fight against these natural impulses and speak up about how we are feeling. Speaking out is extremely important because the narcissist is going to take your silence as an acceptance of their behavior or the words that they have said to you. When you tell them how they are making you feel, you will force them to hear the pain that they are causing you, whether they want to take responsibility for it or not.

It is important that you are honest with yourself, as well. If you have tried to open up to the narcissist and if you have tried to explain to them that they are causing you pain, but they refuse to change, you have done everything in your power, and you should accept that.

If you choose to stay in a relationship with the person, it is going to come at a very high price. Be honest with yourself when you ask yourself these two questions:

> 1. Am I staying in this relationship because I feel that they are doing everything within their power to change?

> 2. Am I staying in this relationship because I am afraid that it is going to be too hard for me to leave?

The narcissist may truly want to change, but that does not mean that you have to continue to endure the same pain over and over again. You can remove yourself from the situation and choose to be happy.

Narcissists have a way of getting under our skin. We naturally respond by either pushing back at them or pulling away from them. That is exactly what they want. It is this chaos and drama that they feed off of. When you let them see what they are doing, the damage that they are causing, you are allowing them not only to hear you but to change. If they are unable to understand your pain, the chances are that they never will. It is sad, and it can be very difficult, but you have to take care of yourself, and sometimes this means ending the relationship.

We have options when it comes to dealing with a narcissist. The first option is to remove the person from your life.

In Intimate Relationships

1. Just stop trying to understand them, stop accepting their behavior, stop letting them take advantage of you, and completely cut them out of your life. Most people are going to tell you that the best way for you to deal with a narcissist is to cut them out of your life completely. That may be true for some, but it does not have to be true for all. However, a narcissist is going to do whatever they can to ensure that every moment of your life is dedicated to serving them in some way. No one deserves to live that way.

If you feel as if you are stuck in a relationship with a narcissist, you can end it. You should not feel any shame when it comes to ending a relationship where you have to endure the abuse of a narcissist. No one has the right to abuse you in any way, shape, or form, and you do not have to continue with the relationship.

2. Do not allow the narcissist to violate your boundaries. If they have in the past, it is time for you to build those boundaries back up and make it very clear to them that you will not allow them to violate the boundaries again.

While the best thing that you could do is to remove them from your life, when it is not possible, such as when they are your family, you may decide that you want to distance yourself from them. There are going to be times when you cannot distance yourself from the narcissist. For example, if your boss is the narcissist that you have to deal with, you will not be able to cut them out of your life or distance yourself from them. You could choose to switch jobs; for now, though, let's assume that you are going to stay at your job.

If your boss is the narcissist that you are dealing with, you are going to have to be able to separate work life from home life. Even if the person is not your boss but just someone that you work with, you need to make sure that you do not let them know anything about your life outside of work. When narcissists at work start learning about our home lives, they begin collecting information about us that they can use against us later. Maintaining your boundaries is going to be worth it because it can save you a lot of headaches down the road.

3. Honesty is the best policy. Narcissists are pros at playing games. Because they are so good at playing these games, you may find yourself tempted to play along with their games. Do not play along! Their behavior will hurt your life or your job. If they are behaving unacceptably, make sure that you let them know. If it is possible, walk away from the situation. If the narcissist is your boss or is someone that you work with, let them know that their behavior is not acceptable then turn the focus back on to whatever it is that you needed from them in the first place.

When you call them out and let them know that their behavior is not acceptable, you will not change what they do or the fact that they are a narcissist, but it will reduce the negativity when you do have to interact with them.

4. When you assess the situation, make sure that you are honest with yourself about what is really going on. Everyone behaves selfishly on occasion, but not everyone is selfish. When a person is a narcissist, they do not behave selfishly on occasion, but they are selfish people. You should never just assume that someone is a narcissist simply because they have behaved selfishly once or twice. Remember, the person could

simply be having a terrible day, or they may have just gotten out of a terrible relationship where they were abused, and they have decided to take some time to put themselves first.

5. Refuse to engage in the narcissist's drama. Narcissists are emotional vampires. For them to feed, they have to cause drama. Never react to their behavior no matter how much it escalates. Never give any attention to their behavior. The more attention that you give to their behavior, the more it will escalate. They will do whatever they can to ensure that you are taking care of them. Once they have sucked you dry, they are going to toss you to the side and find a new victim to feed off of. They are going to do everything within their power to make you believe that everything bad that happens is completely your fault. Being blamed can cause you to lose your cool if you wear your heart on your sleeve.

When you react to a narcissist's behavior, you are communicating to them that you will tolerate their behavior. Everyone has a bad day now and then, and everyone will need support from their friends from time to time. However, when someone has a bad day every day and needs constant support from you, the relationship could be toxic. If the person has narcissistic traits and is constantly asking for your support, you need to protect yourself and make sure that you are not engaging in their drama.

6. Respond politely to the narcissist. Passive aggressiveness is not usually something that is recommended, but when you are dealing with a narcissist, this could be your best option. When they start calling you names, putting you down and then acting as if they are doing you a favor by letting you know all of your flaws, all you have to do is smile and tell them, "Thank you." Or tell them that you appreciate their advice. Even though you do not appreciate what they are saying to you, what you are showing them is that you are not going to allow their words to upset you or your life. A

narcissist uses name-calling and put-downs as a way to make you feel inferior to them. It increases their sense of superiority, and if they get a dramatic reaction from you, they can feed off of the negativity. When you politely respond to them, they will become bored with you and start looking for another victim.

In Family Relationships

Being in an intimate relationship with a narcissist is one thing, but when they are part of your family, it is something else altogether. You have been exposed to their behavior all of your life, and you have no way of removing them from your life. However, there are things that you can do to help you deal with the narcissist to whom you are related.

1. Accept that they are a narcissist and move on with your life. You have to accept the fact that you are not going to be able to fix or cure the narcissist. The narcissist is never going to become the person that you hope they will. They are only going to continue causing you pain. Distancing yourself from the person is the best place to start. This will allow you to understand that you cannot change them.

2. You may want to call them out and tell them that they are a narcissist, but the chances are that this will backfire and only make things worse than what they are. When you tell someone that they are a narcissist, you are probably doing it to try to make them stop what they are doing. However, a narcissist is not able to reflect upon their behavior. Instead of stopping what they are doing, they are going to decide that their goal is to prove you wrong. They are going to become convinced that you are the person that has the problem. Telling someone that they are a narcissist is going to cause problems within your relationship, and it can give them even more of a reason to make your life miserable. They are not

going to stop until you apologize for what you have said and admit that you are the one with the problem.

3. Narcissistic people tend to feel that the entire world has done them wrong. They believe that everyone treats them unfairly. They also believe that they are not being given the respect that they deserve. The narcissist cannot see how their behavior causes people to avoid them or to criticize them. If you have a family member who is always complaining about how hard their life is and how they never get a fair chance, don't feed into their negativity. Instead, tell them, "I hate that you feel that way. Maybe you should put your energy into something else. You always have a choice in life." You can end by telling them good luck.

Doing this may also help you to remember that you have choices in life as well. You can choose to distance yourself from the narcissist or limit the amount of time that you spend together. If you can't distance yourself, a good idea would be to bring another person along when you have to be around the narcissist. Having a third person to witness their behavior usually helps to reduce the behavior.

4. Find someone to support you. Most of the time, when a person is dealing with a narcissistic person, their self-esteem begins to crumble due to all of the criticism, humiliation, and insults. When you have suffered so much abuse, you are going to need some extra support. You can get this from going to therapy, from other members of your family, and from your friends. Be open about your experiences; you should never be ashamed of falling victim to a narcissist.

In the Workplace

The above techniques are all great techniques to use if you are in a relationship with a narcissist or if you are related to a narcissist. But most of them are not going to be of much help if you work with the narcissist or if the narcissist is your boss. Don't worry; there are things that you can do to deal with a narcissist in the workplace.

- Make sure that you get everything in writing when you are dealing with a narcissist at work. If they try to give you instructions verbally, request that they email you the instructions. Make sure that you can document everything possible. You can ask them to send it to you in an email "so you don't forget". You can print these documents out, making sure that you include the time and date that you received them. If they begin causing problems at work or claiming that they told you to do one thing when they actually told you to do something else, you will have documentation to prove what really happened.

- Do not ever fight with them. Avoid fighting as much as possible when you are at work. A narcissist at work is going to do whatever they can to cause you problems, and that could include getting you fired. Do not allow them to cause problems for you. A narcissist is going to seek out your weakness and exploit it. They will find anything that you are sensitive about and use it against you. For example, if they have seen a picture of your children sitting on your desk, and you make them angry, they may make sure that you hear them having a conversation about how terrible a parent you are. They know that when they start questioning the things that you love in life or your most important roles, you will react. They will use that reaction to start causing problems for you.

- Remind yourself that the attack is not personal. It may seem very personal when a person at work is attacking you but remember that a narcissist will attack anyone at work when they perceive that person as better than they are. They are attacking because of their own personal insecurities. When you know this, it can make it easier for you to walk away from the drama that they are trying to cause.

• The narcissist may come to you and tell you that they want to talk to you in private. If they do this, you need to make sure that you do not allow it to happen. Make sure that you bring a witness with you. This will help ensure that the narcissist thinks twice about what they plan on saying to you and abusing you. When you have a witness, it also means that while the narcissist may try to go to your superior and tell them lies, you will have someone that will be able to back up your version of events.

• Avoid contact with the person as much as possible. Avoidance can be the hardest of all of the techniques. However, it is the best one to use if you want to ensure that you do not get caught up in their games. If you do have to interact with the person while you are at work, make sure that you stick to the facts. Get exactly what you need from them or provide them with what they need and end the interaction as quickly as possible.

• You can talk to your boss about the narcissist if they are someone that you have to work with regularly, or you can pay a visit to human resources. Some people may go as far as requesting a transfer due to the abuse that they suffer at the hands of a narcissist at work. You do not have to allow this behavior to continue. You may find that there have been other reports made about this person, or you could find that you are the first. If you find that you are the first person to make a report about the narcissist abusing you, it is probably because they have everyone else too scared to speak up. Be that voice that is needed to tell the narcissist that their behavior is not okay.

• Do not let the narcissist have the satisfaction of knowing that they are getting to you. Do not react to their abuse or try to lash out at them in retaliation. If the narcissist thinks that they are not causing you pain or drama in your life, they will likely move on to the next victim. If they can see that they are causing problems for you at work or home, they are going to continue with their behavior. When a narcissist cannot get a response from someone, they quickly become bored with that person and are forced to find a different target. Remind yourself that you did nothing to warrant this type of abuse, and you do not have to allow it to affect you.

Remember that harassment of any form is a violation of your rights as an employee, even if the person harassing you is your boss. You can visit the EEOC website if you need to get into contact with labor attorneys to discuss your case.

Before you decide to talk to a labor attorney, you may want to consider following the chain of command. If the person who is harassing you is your boss, consider talking to their boss. Report the harassment, ensuring that you have documentation to back up your claims, as well as witnesses. Remember, it is the goal of the narcissist to make you dislike your job so much that you leave it. They feel threatened by your presence in the workplace, and they are doing everything within their power to remove that threat. Do not allow them that satisfaction. Do not allow them to be successful.

While it would be wonderful if we could avoid narcissists, not all of us can. You may be related to the narcissist, or in a relationship with them or you may work with them. By using the techniques that we have gone over in this chapter, you can reduce the damage that the narcissist does in your life. You can take control back from the narcissist.

If you have been the victim of a narcissist in the workplace, you should consider talking to a therapist. Being the victim of any type of abuse is damaging, and it is beneficial to have someone on your side who knows how to help you recover.

Chapter Nine: Why We Love Narcissists (and How to Stop Falling for Them!)

You know that narcissists are toxic. You know that they are arrogant, self-centered, and manipulative. Yet you continue to keep falling in love with them. Studies have shown that even though we know the narcissist is bad for us, we are attracted to their personality, the fact that they can take control of any situation, and we can even be attracted to their hostility.

When we look at a narcissist, we see someone who is strong and outspoken; we see them as someone charming, interesting, and the life of the party. Of course, that is what they want us to see when we first meet them.

Narcissists are extremely popular, much more than other people. Their sense of authority is highly appreciated. They are seen as leaders by those around them. The tone of voice that they use can attract you to them, as well as the way they have mastered their facial movements, and you will usually find yourself attracted to their physical appearance.

When you first meet a narcissist, you will most likely be drawn to their ability to use facial expressions to appear extremely confident. It is not only their facial expressions that screams confidence to us, but it is also the clothes that they wear, their haircut, and their fun personality.

Of course, these assumptions are made off of the first impressions that the narcissist gives off. Later, when we get to know them better, they show us who they really are. The narcissist will cover up their tendencies when you first meet them to draw you in and gain your trust.

Narcissists can thrive in the dating environment because they care about how they look. Of course, we know that a narcissist will care far too much about how they look, but when you first start dating someone, you find this attractive. A person's physical appearance has a huge impact on whether we choose to date them. We live in a world where appearance is very important. Even simple pictures that are posted on social media have to be cropped, and filters added before we will allow the world to see them. Because we find physical appearance so important, we tend to be more attracted to people who focus a lot on their physical appearance.

Narcissists are very good at selling themselves. They know how to make people look up to them and how to make themselves look good. You may also find that you are attracted to them because of their confidence. While we already know that this confidence is nothing more than a mask that the narcissist wears, it can be hard to determine whether it is real or fake at the beginning of the relationship.

Every day narcissists start their morning by looking in the mirror and telling themselves how wonderful they are. All of that practice has allowed them to convince themselves that they are the best, so it makes it very easy for them to convince you of the same thing.

These are only minor traits when it comes to the main reason that a narcissist does so well in the dating field. Being an extrovert and focusing on physical appearance is great, but the thing that narcissists do that draws most people in is their flattery. By providing their potential victim with compliments, gifts, and attention, it looks as if they are enamored of them. When a person comes across as trying to create a healthy relationship, they can gain the trust of the person they are dating.

Sadly, what is happening most of the time is that they are just probing you for information. It may seem as if they are trying to learn as much about you as they can; they are. They are trying to learn everything they can about you. However, they are doing it so that they can use it against you later.

You can start asking them questions, shifting the focus on to them, which is going to slow them down when it comes to collecting information about you, and it is going to allow you to determine whether or not the person that you are seeing is a narcissist. If you tell them, for example, that you love to go hiking and they tell you that they do as well, you can start asking questions about where they like to go hiking, why they enjoy it and so on. Try to make your questions as detailed as possible because this is how you will find out if they are lying.

It is very easy for someone to tell you that they like the same things that you do, but when you start asking them about it, you may find out that they are not as interested as they pretended or that they know nothing about it at all. What many people find when they start asking narcissists questions is that the narcissist is caught off guard and suddenly less attracted to them.

When you are in a relationship, it is just as important for you to get to know the person that you are seeing as it is for them to get to know you. Asking them questions should not be something that makes them turn away from you unless they have a hidden agenda.

As you move into a relationship with a person or as you start dating them, you want to make sure that you do not tell them anything about yourself that you would not tell your boss. People tend to overshare early on in the relationship, but as you already know, the narcissist is focused on gathering as much information about you as they can so that they can use it against you later. Not only can this information be used against you, but it is going to provide the narcissist with a sense of intimacy that does not exist between the two of you.

In a relationship, we share personal information about ourselves in an attempt to become close to other people. A narcissist will use this technique to get very close to you very quickly. Generally speaking, it is never a good idea for two people to become very close very quickly. The narcissist will start sharing what we would consider private information because they know there is a natural urge within us to share information that is on the same level as what has been shared with us. They know that when they open up to us, we may end up opening up to them as well, providing them with information that they can hold over our heads later.

Have you ever met someone, gone on a date or two, and suddenly found yourself in a relationship not quite understanding how it happened? That is what a narcissist will do. They will jump right into a relationship from the very start. If they tell you that they are worried that you are going to break up with them or that you are not going to stick around, the red flags should start going up. The narcissist will use this technique to gain reassurance from you. They want to know that you are too desperate to leave the relationship, even if it is a bad one.

They may tell you that they have to leave town soon, in an attempt to find out if you are willing to commute or even move to where they are going to be relocating. Remind yourself that you are not in a serious relationship with this person. The relationship is in its early stages and does not warrant any type of commitment to the person. Narcissists are great at isolating people, and this could be exactly what they are trying to do. By getting you to move to a new town, they are ensuring that you have no one to turn to and that you are stuck with them. Do not allow the other person to rush you when it comes to the pace of the relationship. Make it clear that you are going to move at a pace that you are comfortable with.

Narcissists are notorious for love bombing, which means that they pour a huge amount of love out on you to get you to do what they want you to do. The narcissist is great at making you feel that they are taking care of you. They will make you feel that they adore you, but the truth is that what they are doing has nothing to do with how much they love you. Instead, it has to do with the narcissist getting what they want out of you by using techniques that they know will work.

If you suspect that the person you are in a relationship with is using love bombing, start paying attention to what they are getting out of the situation. Tell them that you would like for them to slow down and that the relationship is moving too fast for you. Let them know that you want to take the time to get to know each other before plans for the future or any promises are made.

See how the other person reacts. If they respect your wishes, the chances are that they really are a good person and are just very enthusiastic about the relationship. On the other hand, if they are a narcissist, they will continue to use love bombing to get what they want from you.

If the other person does not stop, if they continue to move at a pace that you are not comfortable with, be very firm and tell them to stop. Then get away from them. Don't go back to them just because they promise you that they will slow down. I promise you they will not.

Don't allow yourself to be caught up in some fantasy; the narcissist may look like Prince Charming, but he is nothing more than a heartbreaker.

Another technique that a narcissist will use when you are dating them or in a relationship with them is that they will want to occupy all of your time. They will want you focused completely on them. Have an hour-long lunch break at work? They'll show up. Are you spending the evening at home focusing on self-care? They'll call multiple times to find out what you are doing, even asking if you have other people there with you. Want to go out with your friends for the evening? The narcissist will throw a fit, try to start a fight, and even show up to surprise you. They will do whatever they can to keep you from spending time with your friends and your family.

That is not enough for the narcissist, though. They do not want any of your attention focused anywhere but on them. Have hobbies? When you get into a relationship with a narcissist, you won't have them any longer. Want to pursue your interests? When you are in a relationship with a narcissist, you don't have time to focus on your own interests because you are too busy making sure that they are happy.

How can you tell if the person you are dating is a narcissist? Tell them that you are going to the movie with your friends. They will start asking all sorts of questions. What friends are you going with? What movie are you going to see? What theatre are you going to? (chances are they will show up with or without you knowing). What are you doing after the movie? Turn your phone off and watch them lose their minds. It is likely that when the movie is over, and you turn your phone back on, the notifications from them will go crazy.

Don't answer all of the questions that they ask. Instead, be vague. "Oh, we haven't decided on what movie yet. What theatre? Hmm, I forget which one they said we are going to. Which friends? Oh, just some old friends I've known forever, you don't know them." See how that works? You have let them know that you have heard their question, but you have also shown them that you are not going to answer them. This will make a narcissist lose their minds, and they will not want to be in any type of relationship with you.

The narcissist wants you all to themselves. When the narcissist can separate you from all of the people that you care about, they can start controlling you. Having even one person in your life that cares about you and that you can turn to makes it very hard for the narcissist to take control of you. If you are in a healthy, loving relationship, your partner is going to want you to have friends and hobbies of your own. They are going to want you to do things that make you happy.

Narcissists love to move quickly, and they may try to move in with you right away. If they know that you are not going to let them move in, they may start talking about "sleepovers" very early on in the relationship. This should be a huge bright red flag.

If you are on a date very early on in the relationship and the other person starts talking about sleeping over at your place that night, simply say something like, "Oh sorry, I have plans with my friends after our date." Let them know that they cannot stay at your place. This is very important for you to do. A narcissist knows that if they can get you to live with them, they will be able to take control of your entire life.

When two people move in together too quickly, there is no balance in the relationship. You go from being single to feeling as if you are stuck with this person for the rest of your life. There is no time for the relationship to grow; this is not natural. Humans do not want to spend all of their time alone, which is why we have marriage in the first place. However, when you jump into a serious relationship spending all of your time together too quickly, you are not allowing the relationship to grow naturally.

One of the reasons that so many people move in with someone too quickly is because they have a deep need to be a caretaker. Resist that need to start taking care of that person you do not really know. If you have just met someone or you have just started a new relationship with them, it is not your job to take care of them.

Understandably, you may feel the desire to do so. The narcissist may play off of your sympathy. They might tell you that they recently lost their job; they are out of money and are not going to have a place to live, or that they don't have anywhere to go since they ended their relationship with their ex. They may tell you that their family refuses to help them out, and they have no one to turn to.

If the person tells you that they just left a terrible relationship and they don't have anyone to turn to, let them know that you will not be anyone's rebound and move on with your life. You do not want to risk getting hurt by being the rebound. If they tell you that their family will not help them out, ask yourself why. Maybe their family knows something about them that you do not.

Stop fighting against your instincts. If your gut says that something is wrong, it is probably wrong. It is natural for us to want to help the downtrodden. We want to pick up the injured and nurse them back to health. We want to help make people whole again. However, this is not how healthy romantic relationships are created. A romantic relationship should be between two adults who are self-sufficient and can take care of themselves on their own. If the person that you are dating is not able to support themselves, the chances are that they are not going to be able to pull their weight in the relationship. They are instead going to take advantage of you and push all of the responsibility off on you.

Everyone likes to dream about the future and make big plans, but if you have just met someone or are just starting a relationship with someone and they are already talking about the future or about being together for the rest of your lives, you need to put the brakes on.

Stating, "We're getting a little ahead of ourselves here," is a good way to do this. If they start talking about moving away, getting a house together, or spending your lives together early on in the relationship, use this phrase to let them know that you are not comfortable talking about these things with them. They need to understand that they are not going to push you into something that you are not ready for.

The goal when you are dating is to find someone that you can have a long-term relationship with, but that does not mean that you have to start making these plans right from the beginning. If you do, the narcissist is going to use this against you later on when you want to end the relationship. "This is what you wanted. I gave you exactly what you ask for, and now you are quitting on us."

When you are out on a date, watch how they treat other people. Does your date spend the entire evening belittling the staff at the restaurant? Do they embarrass the waitress or seem to enjoy making other people feel poorly about themselves? How would you feel if the person you are on a date with treated you the way that they treat the people around you? If they tend to treat other people in a way that makes them feel less important, I can assure you that they are going to do the same thing to you at some point in the relationship.

Find someone kind to other people. Pay attention to how the person that you are with treats waitresses or cashiers. If they are respectful and kind to these people, they are probably a good person, and they will be respectful and kind to you as well.

Meeting a narcissist, being love-bombed, and falling victim to them can happen so quickly that many people do not even notice that it is happening. However, by using these techniques, you can be aware of the very start of the relationship just what kind of person you are dating.

You are going to protect yourself from any abuse or pain at the hands of a narcissist in the future. You are going to be able to ensure that you do not fall victim to a narcissist ever again, and that is great news. The bad news is that while you may like the way that a person portrays themselves, you may find out that they are actually a narcissist, trying to take advantage of you, and you will end up having to walk away from the relationship.

While this is no fun, it is much better than becoming the victim of an abusive narcissist.

Chapter Ten: A Narcissist's Secret Fears

Narcissists put a lot of effort into making others believe that they are very confident and successful. The narcissist may act like they are superior to everyone else. They will boast about how great they are and thrive on the attention that they get. They believe that they are special because only the most important people get this type of attention. The narcissist does not believe that anyone else deserves the type of attention that they get. Ordinary people simply are not worthy of it. To the narcissist being special means that they are not ordinary. They are not like everyone else.

Deep down, the narcissist is actually very fragile. They have fears that they try to hide from everyone around them. By knowing these fears, you can use them against the narcissist to ensure that you do not become their next victim. If you are already the victim of a narcissist, you can use those fears to make them lose interest in you.

    1. The narcissist has flaws. Narcissists believe that they are perfect, and they want everyone else to believe that as well.

This is why when something negative happens, they will blame it on other people. They do not want anyone to perceive them as anything but perfect. If they were not perfect, they would not be special, and they do not want to be known as ordinary. The narcissist will not want to admit that because they are human, they will make mistakes and have imperfections. They do not want to admit to experiencing self-doubt because this could make them seem weak.

A narcissist will become offended by simple truths that affect all humans, such as everyone has limitations, everyone suffers loss at some point in their lives, no one can do everything on their own, everyone has flaws, and no one is perfect. The narcissist is constantly on guard, making sure that they are ready for anything that could happen to make them look less than perfect. They will do everything possible to ensure that no one sees their flaws.

While this may sound like an exhausting task, the narcissist will simply project every flaw that they have onto the people around them. What is ironic about this situation is that a person who is what the narcissist would define as superior would never need to build themselves up by putting other people down.

Knowing that the narcissist is terrified of their flaws being revealed can be very freeing. Knowing what they are afraid of can help you to understand why their rage has been triggered.

2. Narcissists are terrified of being in a real relationship. This is not to say that a narcissist will not be in any relationship but that they will not commit themselves to a relationship. You have already learned that a narcissist will not let their guard down. When you enter a real relationship, or when you choose to be committed to a relationship, letting your guard down is a necessity. Being in a committed relationship means

that you have to let the other person see who you really are. A narcissist cannot do this.

A narcissist knows that if they allow someone to get too close to them, their insecurities will be exposed. They know that the person that they are in a relationship with is going to learn all of their secrets, and a narcissist cannot allow that to happen.

3. Self-reflection is a very important part of self-improvement, but this is something that a narcissist cannot take part in. The narcissist is in denial about who they really are, and one of their biggest fears is having to face that. The narcissist wants to believe that they are perfect, but they know that if they practice self-reflection, they are going to have to face their flaws, insecurities, and other issues that they do not want to deal with.

4. While a narcissist can dish out insults one right after the other, they are unable to handle being insulted. Narcissists can spend all day criticizing other people, but when this criticism is turned back on them, they cannot handle it. The majority of narcissists do not have as much confidence and self-esteem as they want you to believe. In fact, their egos are very fragile. Because of this, when they are insulted, it devastates them and takes a huge toll on their already low self-confidence.

5. A narcissist does not experience guilt when they hurt another person; therefore, this is not a concern for them, but what they are afraid of is shame. The shame that the narcissist is afraid of is the feeling of being unworthy.

6. One of the biggest fears that a narcissist will have is a lack of admiration. A narcissist is much like a performer. They want the spotlight to be on them all of the time, but more than that, they want everyone to admire them. They are willing to go to great lengths to get the admiration of other

people. The narcissist is going to take extreme measures to impress other people, and they fear that those attempts will be ignored.

7. A narcissist fears being exposed for what and who they truly are. Narcissists tell lies all of the time. They may end up telling so many lies that they are unable to keep up with them all. They may lie about past relationships, experiences that they have had in life, their family, childhood, or their accomplishments. They use these lies to impress the people around them or to manipulate their victims into doing what they want them to do. The narcissist knows that by telling these lies, they are going to be able to get what they want from the people around them but deep down, they are terrified that they are going to be exposed. They are afraid that people will begin to compare notes about them, and that they will be called out on the lies that they have told. They are afraid that people will learn the truth about them.

8. To a narcissist, expressing gratitude means that they were dependent upon another person. Because the narcissist does not want anyone to think that they need them, they are unable to express gratitude. Saying thank you is almost impossible for a narcissist to do. They do not want anyone to know that they need help, and they refuse to admit that they do. Showing gratitude, even by saying "thank you", goes against everything that a narcissist is.

9. The narcissist fears death. The narcissist thinks of themselves as untouchable. In their opinion, nothing bad could ever happen to them. They believe that no matter what it is that they do, they will be successful at it. They have what is known as a god complex. Everyone knows that no matter how powerful, how successful, or how superior a person is, none of us can avoid death. Because of this, the narcissist will suffer a lot of distress whenever they think about death. This is the one thing in their life that they have no power

over. They are not able to control it, and they know that it could happen at any time. Death is their biggest threat.

Most importantly, the narcissist is afraid of their victims becoming strong. They are afraid that they are going to lose their power over you. They know that there is a chance that you will empower yourself with knowledge, learn about their techniques, and start seeing through the façade that they have created. They know that if you do this, you are going to quickly begin to realize that you do not have to allow them to control you any longer. They will no longer be able to get from you what they want, which was why they had you in their life in the first place. When you stop responding to their behavior and start living the life that you want to live, they panic. When you take control away from them, you show them that they no longer matter, they are unimportant, and there is nothing special about them. Sure, they can replace you easily enough and find another victim to feed off of, but knowing that they were not important to you, knowing that you were able to walk away from them no matter how much they tried to manipulate you will eat at them for the rest of their lives.

Chapter Eleven: Can a Narcissist Change?

Being in a relationship with a narcissist - whether it be at work, in a family, or in a romantic relationship - can be confusing. The relationship can become manipulative as well as abusive. Not every relationship with every narcissist will turn abusive. However, it is good to be aware that this could happen. It is also important to understand that narcissism is not a disorder. Narcissism is a trait that people have. Narcissistic Personality Disorder or NPD is a disorder that must be treated by a professional. A person can display narcissistic traits without having NPD.

Many people believe that it is impossible for anyone who displays narcissistic traits to change. The truth is that a person who is displaying narcissistic traits can change. While this change is not easy, it is possible. Once the narcissist starts focusing on the change, addressing the insecurities and loneliness that they have tried so hard to hide, they can even start to feel empathy.

Feeling empathy can be very difficult for a recovering narcissist to do. However, it is possible. To feel empathy, they are going to have to give up their need to feel superior to other people. For a narcissist to change, certain things have to occur.

First, there has to be some type of consequence to the narcissist that is meaningful to them. For example, they may lose their job or the people that they love if they do not change. One huge motivator for a narcissist to change is damage to their reputation. They may also be motivated to change if they feel that they are missing out on opportunities in their life.

They may also be motivated by the positive effects that the change will bring into their lives. For example, they will not have as many fallouts in their personal or work relationships. The relationships will begin to improve and normalize.

Therapy is something that the narcissist will need. The emotions that they have tried to hide for so long must be addressed. This is why they need to see a good therapist. You may have a strong desire to help the narcissist change, but a therapist has the training to help them do so. The therapist is going to be able to hold the narcissist accountable for their actions while not being vulnerable to their rage. If you are in a relationship with a narcissist, you will want to seek therapy as well. The two of you may also choose to take part in therapy that focuses on the relationship, apart from your personal therapy.

It is worth mentioning that some narcissists are not going to see the need to change. There are times when it does not matter what the narcissist is at risk of losing; they will not admit that they have faults or have done anything wrong. If they refuse to admit to any wrongdoings, while they need help, the chances are that they are not going to seek it out.

The following steps are going to help the narcissist change their behavior:

1. Become aware of other people's boundaries and start being considerate of them.

The narcissist tends to be unaware of where they end, and another person begins. Therefore, for them to start seeing other people as humans instead of possessions, they will want to start becoming aware of the boundaries that are set by other people.

They can do this by starting to address other people by their names when they are speaking to them and when they are writing.

The narcissist is known to demand attention all of the time, which means that when they are around other people go unheard. The narcissist should focus on listening to what other people are saying. While other people are talking, they should show interest in what is being said. The narcissist misses out on a lot of opportunities to learn about life because they never listen to other people's personal experiences.

When the narcissist wants someone to do something for them, they will need to start making requests instead of making demands. They have to give the other person the space that they need to make their own choices instead of meeting the demands of the narcissist. Once they make their choice, the narcissist must respect it and not try to force the person to do what was requested of them.

2. Develop and Deliver

The narcissist is used to cheating, lying, manipulating, exaggerating, taking short cuts, not keeping commitments, and breaking promises. For them to create genuine relationships, they will have to start building trust with the people around them.

This means that they have to do what they say they are going to do. They will have to learn how to keep their promises, follow through on commitments, and keep their agreements and appointments. The best way to do this is to make sure that they are not making promises that they are not going to be able to keep. One huge mistake that narcissists and non-narcissists make is making promises or commitments that they know they are not going to be able to keep.

When the narcissist is not able to follow through with their commitments, they need to be held accountable for their actions.

They also need to take the time to identify what they can do to ensure that this does not happen again. It is also very important for them to figure out what they can do to make things right with the person that they broke the promise to. This will help them learn that they are accountable for their actions.

3. Become More Mindful

Mindfulness allows one to focus on what is going on right now. For example, if you are doing eighty down the interstate, and it suddenly starts to snow, being mindful of the situation can help you quickly become aware that you need to slow down. If you were not mindful of the situation, but were instead focusing on your plans for tomorrow, you might find yourself sliding off the side of the road before you realize what is going on.

How does this help the narcissist? They can ask themselves questions like, "How is this going to be perceived by the person I am speaking to?" Or, "Am I trying to make myself look or feel superior to those around me?" Being mindful will allow the narcissist to become more aware of their actions, which in turn will help them change the behavior before someone gets hurt.

4. Ask for Help

Earlier in this book, you learned that it is very difficult for a narcissist to ask for help. They do not want to be seen as someone that depends on other people. However, by asking for help or support as they make these changes in their lives, they are going to increase their self-confidence and feel like they really belong. Instead of the illusion that people like them, they will start to see what it is like to have people care about them. Narcissists are usually very lonely because they do not let anyone get too close to them. We already talked about how they are afraid that by letting someone get too close, they will be exposed for what they really are.

If the narcissist is seriously trying to change, they should open up to at least one person in their lives. As time goes on, they will be able to open up to more and more people. Support groups are a good option for the narcissist who is afraid to open up to people and can be a small step in the right direction.

5. Forgive Themselves

As the narcissist starts to make changes in their life, they may begin to feel remorse for the pain that they have inflicted upon other people. This is completely natural; however, the narcissist may begin to think of themselves as a bad person. They will begin feeling guilt that they never felt before. This can cause them to wallow in guilt and even become depressed. It is extremely important at this point that the narcissist forgives themselves for the things that happened in the past. They may need to be reminded that the past has no bearing on what happens today. The past cannot be changed, but their future can. Do not continually bring the past up, throwing it in the narcissist's face, trying to make them feel bad about what they did. If they reach this point of change, they already feel bad enough. Instead, show them forgiveness so that they can forgive themselves.

As the narcissist works to make these changes in their life, they will return to humanity. They will be more authentic, and they are going to have much healthier relationships. They will see themselves accomplishing things that they never thought possible, and their self-confidence will be real. Soon they will begin to understand that they can make themselves feel good about who they are, and they don't have to use other people to feel that way.

Change does not happen overnight. It can take a very long time for a narcissist to be able to put all of the narcissistic traits behind them. However, as long as they continue to work toward their goal and be honest with themselves, change is possible.

Once the change has happened, it is not time to stop. Continually learning and working to improve oneself will help the narcissist create the life that they truly want. This will help them to experience true happiness and become real again.

The narcissist may have experiences for the first time that make them uncomfortable. They may experience what it is like to be hurt by another person, to be vulnerable, and to admit that they have flaws. This can be very difficult to deal with at first, and you should be prepared for some struggle. There may be times when the narcissist just wants to give up. It is so much easier for them to continue to manipulate people to get what they want in life than it is for them to work toward improving themselves and creating that life on their own.

Continue to provide support for the narcissist as long as they continue to work toward making these changes. If they are having a particularly hard time dealing with the emotions that they are going to face, remind them why they decided to make the change in the first place.

It can be hard for you as the narcissist makes these changes as well. You have already spent so much of your time trying to heal the people you harmed and trying to do whatever you could to make them happy. You may feel completely drained and as if you have nothing else to give to them, which is why you need to seek help for yourself.

Chapter Twelve: Exposing Emotional Abuse

While not everyone that has narcissistic traits has Narcissistic Personality Disorder, they can develop it. Today we hear people throwing the word narcissistic around all of the time. You may have seen it all over social media. If you have tried to do any research on emotional abuse, you may have found an overwhelming number of websites talking about narcissism. While it may feel good to give your abuser a title, it is important to make sure that this is what they are actually suffering from. Only a professional can diagnose NPD.

Some of the people who are abusive towards their partners are narcissistic, but some of them are not. Some of them are dealing with other mental disorders; some of them do not have any mental disorders whatsoever. The fact is that nothing has shown that there is a link between mental disorders and abuse.

Even if you have no idea why the person that you are with is emotionally abusing you, you need to expose the abuse. One problem that many people come across when they connect the abuse with a mental disorder is that they feel as if there is nothing that can be done about it. They accept the abuse because that is just how the person is. It makes them feel that they have no control over the situation and that they must deal with it.

Some people may start to believe that if they could only get a diagnosis for their partner, the abuse would stop. If only the partner took medication for the disorder, they would not have to suffer the abuse any longer. Sadly, medication is not the answer. Medication can treat mental disorders, but it is not going to change abusive behavior. The abuse would have to be addressed separately from the mental disorder.

Abusing someone is a choice that is made by the abuser. People who are suffering from mental disorders are not always in control of the choices that they make, so that sort of abuse could improve with the treatment of a mental disorder, though this is rarely the case.

An abusive partner can control their behaviors such as choosing to push limits to see how much they can get away with. For example, it may start as verbal abuse, but then they slap their partner to see if they can get away with it. The person is in control of the way that they behave if they are only abusive towards you. Do they have the ability to treat other people with respect? If this is the case, they are choosing to be abusive.

They may also choose to intensify the abuse as time goes on. A person who has a mental disorder will generally behave the same way most of the time. However, an abusive person's behavior will escalate as the relationship progresses.

You need to understand that whether your partner has a mental disorder or not, they do not have the right to abuse you in any way. You are never going to be able to fix them or get them to change their behavior. It is your responsibility to stand up for yourself and start taking action.

Abuse can take on many different forms. One of those forms is emotional abuse. Because there are no physical signs of emotional abuse, it can be hard to detect. When many people think of emotional abuse, they tend to believe that it is not as serious as physical abuse. However, it is just as dangerous and can cause a lot of damage to the victim.

Emotional abuse can lead to the victim suffering from PTSD, depression, anxiety, low self-esteem, and a low sense of self-worth.

Before we go into how you can get help, let's go over a few *myths* that people tend to believe about emotional abuse.

1. Many people believe that *emotional abuse and physical abuse always happen together*. The truth is that a person can be a victim of emotional abuse without ever being a victim of physical abuse. This is what makes it so hard for those outside of the relationship to spot.

2. *Women are the victims of emotional abuse*. Emotional abuse is like any other type of abuse, and men, as well as women, can fall victim to it. Emotional abuse usually happens within a romantic relationship, but it can also occur in families or between friends.

3. *Emotional abuse isn't as bad as physical abuse*. All abuse is hurtful. Comparing one type of abuse to another type of abuse is absurd. No one has the right to judge the amount of pain that a victim has experienced and claim that another form of abuse is worse. Abuse is abuse. No matter what type of abuse you are experiencing, you deserve to be free from it.

Sign of Emotional Abuse

Do you think that you could be the victim of emotional abuse? If you suspect that you are emotionally abused, it is time for you to reach out for help. Asking for help is one of the bravest things that you will ever do. There is help out there for you.

There are many different ways for you to reach out for help:

• Go to someone that you trust and tell them what is going on. If you go to church, this could be your pastor. You can go to a trusted friend or another family member. If you are a minor, find an adult you trust, for instance, a teacher or the principal at your school, and talk to them about what is going on. Tell whoever you go to that you need to speak to them privately, which is going to allow them to really hear what you are saying, and it will provide you with a safe environment. It can be very hard to talk to another person about the abuse that you have been experiencing. Tell them as much as you can without making yourself uncomfortable. Take things as slowly as you need to, but make sure that you are sticking to the facts. Don't worry if you become emotional and break down, they are going to understand, and it is going to provide you with some emotional relief.

• If you are a child who is suffering abuse, call child protective services, or seek out the social worker at your school. You can look online to find the phone number for child-protection services in your state. You do not even have to give them your name when you call. Just tell them what is going on, and they will investigate. A worker, as well as a police officer, will be sent to your home, and they will talk to you privately about the situation.

• Contact the police. If you are in physical danger, call 911 immediately. Do not wait and ask for help later. Do not allow anyone to hurt you. If you are not in immediate danger, you can call the non-emergency number to talk to an officer about a pattern of abuse. If you are the victim, the dispatcher will ask you if you are safe or if you feel safe. After you have talked to the dispatcher, an officer will be dispatched to your location. If you do not want the officer to come to your home, you should go to the police station to give the report. Make sure that you tell the police everything but stick to the facts. You will want to bring any evidence with you to give to the police. Give the police as much information as possible, but if you are unclear about something that they have asked you, don't be afraid to let them know. Finally, make sure that you are available if the police officer needs to follow up. You should never call and ask for updates on the investigation. The police are not going to be able to give you that type of information. If the abuser does end up getting arrested, the prosecutor may contact you asking that you testify against the accused. If you are afraid to do this, you do not have to; no one is going to make you testify.

- Sometimes reaching out to the police can seem overwhelming. If you need to talk to someone, express what you are feeling or if you are unsure that what you are going through is abuse, you can text HELLO to 741741. This will connect you to a crisis counselor. If the abuser has access to your phone, make sure that you delete the messages after the conversation has ended.

- Create a safety plan. Even if you are not suffering from physical abuse, you need to make sure that you have a safety plan. Think of places that you can go to get away from the abuser. Create a plan that you can follow when you are ready to get out of the relationship. Make sure that you know where you will go, who you will contact, and how you will survive. Be as detailed as possible so that when the time comes, you do not have to worry about anything.

Dealing with Emotional Abuse

If you are in an emotionally abusive relationship, remember that you deserve to be treated with respect and love. No one deserves to suffer from abuse. It can take time for you to recover from the abuse that you have suffered. You need to put yourself first and practice self-care.

You can start your recovery by talking to a professional. You are going to need help processing everything that has happened to you and the emotions that come with the abuse. Some therapists have been trained to work specifically with abuse survivors. The therapist is going to be able to teach you how to cope with the abuse and all of your emotions.

Learning how to practice self-care is very important if you have been in any type of abusive relationship. You have been taking care of your abuser for so long that you likely have not been taking care of yourself. Start focusing on you for once, which will help reduce any anxiety or depression that you are dealing with due to the abuse.

Focus on providing your body with the healthy food that it needs, getting enough exercise, reading a book, spending time doing the things that you enjoy the most. Make yourself and your health a priority.

Start building strong and healthy friendships. Don't try to jump into a new relationship while you are healing from an abusive one. Instead, focus on making new friends and finding the right people. Start taking a class, learn something new, or spend some time working on something that you enjoy with a group of people.

Emotional abuse can be very damaging, but there are things that you can do to protect yourself and to take control of your life back. You should never feel that you are stuck in a situation because you are being abused. You can find your way out, and you can live a happy and fulfilling life.

Conclusion: Thriving after a Narcissistic Relationship

Once you have broken free from a narcissistic relationship, you may find it hard to move on. This is not uncommon when a person has been in a relationship with a narcissist.

The narcissist expected special treatment from you whether they did things to deserve this treatment or not. They only way that the narcissist can satisfy their fragile ego is by putting others down. They love to make you feel as if you cannot live without them. I have good news for you. You are not only going to be able to survive without them, but you are going to be able to thrive.

One of the best pieces of knowledge that you can have as you move forward with your life is that the narcissist that you were in a relationship with could not think of anyone else but themselves. They are only focused on what makes them feel good. Chances are you want to make sure that you never end up in another relationship with a narcissist again. How can you do this? By thriving.

Look at it like this; if you had high self-esteem when you met the narcissist, the chances are that they would not have been interested in you. The narcissist wants to be in a relationship with someone that they can control, someone that is going to make them feel superior. If a person has a healthy level of self-confidence, they may make the mistake of getting into a relationship with a narcissist, but the relationship will be cut short. They will recognize that there is a problem within the relationship and move on with their life. More importantly than that, they refuse to accept the blame for the relationship not working out. Instead, they understand that the relationship was not working, and they are focused on their own happiness. They are not willing to accept any relationship that adds no value to their lives.

To make sure that you do not end up in another relationship like this again, you will want to start focusing on you. Start by believing in yourself. Focus on creating the life that you want and becoming the person that you want to be. Focus on your career, your dreams, and your hopes. Take the time to finally focus on your health or learning that new skill you have always wanted to learn. Spend time doing the things that you love and building your self-esteem.

Perhaps at some point early on in the relationship, you started to wonder how such an amazing person might have wanted to be with you. That should have been your first clue that something was wrong. When you focus on building your self-confidence, you will never question why someone would want to be with you. If you are working on overcoming your relationship with a narcissist, you need to remember that you are amazing.

Narcissists are very picky about who they date. They want to be with someone successful and accomplished. They also want to be with someone who downplays who they really are. *Now* is the time for you to rise to the top. It is time for you to embrace who you are and move on with your life.

Ask yourself what was it that made the narcissist feel that they could target you. Are you neglecting yourself in an area of your life that makes you an easy target for the narcissist? Are you putting yourself down? Do you feel that other people are better than you are? Do you put other people down so that you can feel better about yourself? Some of the narcissist's traits may be mirrored in you. What you should focus on, however, is what trait is causing the biggest issue for you. How are you allowing that trait to affect your life? Learning from this experience is the best way to make sure that you do not repeat this mistake in the future.

This can be a lot for a person to absorb. Remember, we are not trying to focus on making you feel poorly about yourself. Instead, it is about ensuring that you can thrive in your life while ensuring that you never fall victim to a narcissist again.

You have suffered both mentally and emotionally. This can cause many people to completely collapse and become a victim for the rest of their lives. Some people also turn into abusers themselves because they begin to take on the tendencies of the narcissist. I want better for you.

You don't have to be a victim any longer. Once you have ended the relationship, you can accept that to be true. It is time for you to move forward in your life without abuse.

To do this, you have to stop living in denial. Stop making excuses for the abuse that you suffered. It is easy to try to make excuses for the abuser. You want to feel sorry for them. You want to come up with a reason that they did the things that they did. However, if you want to move forward with your life, you simply have to accept that the abuse happened. Stop dwelling on the details. By dwelling on the details, you are allowing the abuser to continue to affect your life.

Set up boundaries that you will stick to when you enter any new relationships. Make sure that those boundaries are clear and that there are clear consequences to those boundaries being crossed. Knowing what your boundaries are will help you to protect yourself in the future.

Confront the abuse. Do not try to pretend that it did not happen. Do not allow the abuser to convince you that you should stay friends after the end of the relationship. Narcissists will do this to keep you around so that they can take advantage of you later. Confront them. Tell them what they did to you and that their behavior was not acceptable.

When you do confront them, stick to your points, and end the conversation. Narcissists are bullies. They are good at bullying. They can turn the conversation around and place the blame on you, which is one of the ways they are able to keep their victims around for so long.

Cut the narcissist off. Do not have any contact with them after the relationship has ended. If they want to meet up and talk, tell them no. This can be very difficult, but it is the best thing for you.

Finally, you need to move on with your life. Choose to focus on the life that you want and create that life. When you are busy creating the life that you want, you are not going to have time to focus on the abuser or the abuse.

Many people think that it is impossible to move on after they have been in an abusive relationship. They tell themselves that they are always going to be the victim and that they did something to deserve the pain that they endured. You did not do anything to deserve the abuse, and you no longer have to be the victim.

So, start right now. Start focusing on that life that you deserve. Start working on becoming a person whom a narcissist will never target because they know they would not get away with abusing them.